D1602543

Family Portraits

Family Portraits

By
Dr. Raymond Barber

SWORD of the LORD
PUBLISHERS
P. O. Box 1099 • Murfreesboro, TN 37133

Printed and Bound in the United States of America

DEDICATION

This volume of sermons is affectionately dedicated to my wife, Helen, who has been my faithful companion for forty-six years and who has made our house a home. Her expertise in grammar and sentence structure has proven invaluable. Having taught college English for twenty-five years, she is well qualified.

A special thanks to my secretary, Stephanie Houston, who did the transcribing and word processing of the messages in preparation for the publisher.

I am indebted to the congregation of Worth Baptist Church who listened to me preach during my thirty-five years as pastor.

CONTENTS

INTRODUCTION

God is a "family God," and the Bible is a family-oriented Book. Even the casual reader will discern that God, through His inspired Word, stresses the importance of the family and emphasizes its preservation from one generation to the next.

The family is the basic unit of society, and long before the founding of the church, the organization of government, or the establishment of a school or a business, God put the family together, uniting Adam and Eve in matrimony and instructing them to "multiply, and replenish the earth" (Gen. 1:28).

As goes the family, so goes the church; and as goes the church, so goes the nation. No church is more spiritual, stable or solidified than the families that make up its membership. No nation is stronger than the moral fiber of the home and the church.

Being the pastor of the same church for thirty-five years has afforded me the opportunity to witness the development of a second and third generation within the confines of the membership. Family traits and traditions have been handed down from one generation to the succeeding one. Patterns of behavior have been evident as parents have set the example for their children to follow. In some cases this has been prudent and profitable. In others it has been less than desirable.

In the Garden when God performed the first wedding, a precedent was set for the entire human race. There can be no improvement upon God's prescription, and there must be no deviation from it. To transgress the laws of God concerning matrimony and family structure is to invite divine disaster and incur holy wrath.

The book of Genesis is the book of origins, and the establishment of the home is paramount among all God did from the dawn of creation.

The sermons in this book can be thought of as biographies of the men and women whose families have influenced all succeeding generations. They all appear on the stage of human performance in the book of Genesis. Their drama is acted out, and they pass on, but not without influencing the lives of the millions who have read the story over and over again.

Adam, the first man, created in the likeness and image of God, teaches us the consequences of making a deal with the Devil, and we learn it never pays to bargain with Satan. The price to pay is exceedingly high, and every family has felt the blow.

Noah, the first builder of ships, gives us a lesson on the grace of God, who preserves the family in the hour of universal judgment.

Abraham, the friend of God, is seen as the great patriarch whose family is an example of obedience and family togetherness.

Lot, the backslider, proves to be a loser, and from his disastrous life of sorrow we learn how not to design the family structure.

Isaac, a beautiful type of our Lord, gives us a wonderful example of a marriage made in Heaven. Young couples would do well to read again this story and pattern their marriages after it.

Jacob, the "prince with God," after years of wandering

comes back to God and discovers that God's way is the best way for the family to live and love.

Joseph, the son of the old age and a marvelous type of Christ, is seen as the leading player in the drama of a family that suffered a "breakup" but in the end experienced a "makeup" that changes the course of history and inspires all families to "come back together" and live in harmony.

May the God of the family raise a canopy above your home, and as you read these messages may you reevaluate the status of your family. Preserving the family is a **must** in perpetuating truth and holiness.

THE FAMILY THAT MADE A DEAL WITH THE DEVIL

—ADAM—
Genesis 2:18–25

"And the LORD God said, It is not good that the man should be alone; I will make him an help meet for him.

"And out of the ground the LORD God formed every beast of the field, and every fowl of the air; and brought them unto Adam to see what he would call them: and whatsoever Adam called every living creature, that was the name thereof.

"And Adam gave names to all cattle, and to the fowl of the air, and to every beast of the field; but for Adam there was not found an help meet for him.

"And the LORD God caused a deep sleep to fall upon Adam, and he slept: and he took one of his ribs, and closed up the flesh instead thereof;

"And the rib, which the LORD God had taken from man, made he a woman, and brought her unto the man.

"And Adam said, This is now bone of my bones, and flesh of my flesh: she shall be called Woman, because she was taken out of Man.

"Therefore shall a man leave his father and his mother, and shall cleave unto his wife: and they shall be one flesh.

"And they were both naked, the man and his wife, and were not ashamed."

THE HOME IS GOD'S PRIORITY

There are three, and only three, divinely-ordained agencies in our world: the home, the government and the church. The Devil is out to destroy all three. His primary

1

> **The home is the Devil's primary target.**

target is the home, because as goes the home, so goes the church; as goes the church, so goes the government; as goes the government, so goes the nation; as goes the nation, so goes the world. Do not be surprised if Satan launches an all-out attack on your family. Do not sell short the power of Satan. Satan goes to church, and he has to ride with somebody. Wherever God's people come together—just trace it through the Scripture—the Devil is always there. He is out to trick and deceive you.

First, there was the **home** (Gen. 2:24). Then came **government** (Gen. 9:6). The **church** came much later. In Matthew 16:18 Jesus said, ". . . and upon this rock I will build my church." It is plain to see that the home takes precedence over both the government and the church. God's primary institution is the home and the **family**.

Every time I unite a couple in marriage—and I have joined a few in these almost forty years—I have said to them that long before there was a church, a government, a school, a business; long before there was a corporation or any other agency or organization, there was a marriage, a family, a home.

The Home Is Sacred. Do you want to know how sacred marriage is? God Himself performed the first wedding, bringing together the first man, Adam, and the first woman, Eve. And it was not Adam and Steve. God does not accept homosexuality as a lifestyle. The homosexually-related diseases are destroying thousands. The judgment hand of God is upon America because we have gone contrary to His way, His Word and His will.

Make this observation with me. Does it not stand to

reason that the sacredness of the home is evidenced by the fact that it was formed before the government or the church? God could have formed the government before He formed a home. He could have established the church before He established the home. But God's priority was to establish a home on earth.

Jesus Worked in the Home. I list seven things to show you what Jesus thought about the home:

1. Jesus performed His first **miracle** in a home—a wedding in Cana of Galilee (John 2:11).
2. Jesus observed a **Passover** in a home (Matt. 26:18).
3. Jesus ate **supper** in the home of a sinner. Aren't you glad Jesus loves sinners? He is a friend to the sinner, and that makes Him your friend and mine because we are sinners. He went home to eat with a sinner. Of course those hypocritical Pharisees pointed a finger and said, 'Look at Him, associating with sinners!' Had He not, He would have nothing to do with us.
4. Jesus **visited** in the home of a tax-collector, the most despised person in the community (Matt. 9:9–11). Aren't you glad that He has love, time and concern for the most despised people in the world?
5. Jesus was **anointed** with perfume in a home (Mark 14:3). Against His burial, a women broke an alabaster box of perfume worth a whole year's wages, and poured it upon His feet and head.
6. Jesus **healed** a man with palsy in a home (Mark 2:1–5).
7. Jesus **taught** in the home of Mary and Martha (Luke 10:38–43).

I am giving you God's picture of a family in this chapter. We might call Adam's family "the family that made a deal with the Devil."

Please observe three things about the first family:
1. The first family was established by God.
2. The first family disobeyed God's instructions.
3. The first family was struck with tragedy.

GOD ESTABLISHED THE FIRST FAMILY

"And the LORD God said, It is not good that the man should be alone; I will make him an help meet for him" (Gen. 2:18). Hundreds have quoted that verse like this: "God said, 'I am going to make a help mate.'" No; He said, 'I will make a help that is compatible to him.' "Help meet" means a help or helper, a compatible person.

Notice three things in verses 18 to 24: First, there is **companionship**—verse 18: "I will make him an help meet"—a companion, one who is compatible.

A second thing is **relationship**—verse 23: "And Adam said [here is a new relationship that had never existed before], This is now bone of my bones, and flesh of my flesh: she shall be called Woman, because she was taken out of Man." From where was she taken? Out of his head so he could lord it over her? No. From his feet so he could walk on her, trample her? No. From near his heart so there would be a compatibility, a togetherness, a oneness, a love, a companionship, a fellowship.

So there is companionship in verse 18; there is relationship in verse 23. Then in verse 24 there is **partnership**: "Therefore shall a man leave his father and his mother, and shall cleave unto his wife: and they shall be one flesh."

When a man leaves his father and mother, he breaks the closest ties that he has. Do not allow Mother and

Daddy to take the love and affection that your spouse deserves to receive from you. Do not give Mother and Daddy first place. I am not saying to be disrespectful of them, but God said your first obligation is to the one you married. If you could get this straight before walking down the aisle to join hearts and hands and to say "I do," or "I will," then you would be far better off.

God ordained one man and one woman in a lifetime relationship. Here is a principle right out of the Word of God that ought not be violated. If you have had multiple marriages, God still loves you. Divorce does not mean you cannot be forgiven.

> God ordained one man and one woman in a lifetime relationship.

I am reminded of the old maid who wanted a husband so badly. She kept going to her pastor and saying, "Now pastor, you told me to pray for a man; I have prayed but haven't gotten one yet."

The pastor said, "Now look. God has a plan, a program: one man for one woman, and you can't improve on it."

"But pastor, I don't want to improve on it. I just want to get in on it."

In Matthew 19:3–9 Jesus gives us a commentary on what God the Father said in Genesis 2:

"The Pharisees also came unto him, tempting him, and saying unto him, Is it lawful for a man to put away his wife for every cause?

"And he answered and said unto them, Have ye not read, that he which made them at the beginning made them male and female,

"And said, For this cause shall a man leave father and mother, and shall cleave to his wife: and they twain shall be one flesh?

"Wherefore they are no more twain, but one flesh. What therefore God hath joined together, let not man put asunder.

"They say unto him, Why did Moses then command to give a writing of divorcement, and to put her away?

"He saith unto them, Moses because of the hardness of your hearts suffered you [or allowed you] *to put away your wives: but from the beginning it was not so.*

"And I say unto you, Whosoever shall put away his wife, except it be for fornication, and shall marry another, committeth adultery: and whoso marrieth her which is put away doth commit adultery."

God's way, God's Word, God's will, God's plan. Jesus is emphasizing it—verse 9: "And I say unto you, Whosoever shall put away his wife, except it be for fornication, and shall marry another, committeth adultery: and whoso marrieth her which is put away doth commit adultery." God has a principle; don't be offended by the principle laid out in the Word of God.

THE FIRST FAMILY DISOBEYED GOD'S RESTRICTIONS

God has certain restrictions on every family—upon children and upon parents. There is no reason why a Christian family cannot sit down together and work out problems and resolve differences to the glory of God. It is difficult sometimes to do it, but it can be done. The first family disobeyed the restrictions that God placed upon them.

Turn to Genesis 2:15–17:

"And the Lord God took the man, and put him into the garden of Eden to dress it and to keep it.

"And the LORD God commanded the man, saying, Of every tree of the garden thou mayest freely eat:

6

"But of the tree of the knowledge of good and evil, thou shalt not eat of it: for in the day that thou eatest thereof thou shalt surely die."

God says you can have this, you can do this, you can go here, you can go there; but you cannot do this, you cannot have this, you cannot go there, you cannot do that. "Now the serpent was more subtil than any beast of the field which the LORD God had made. And he said unto the woman, Yea, hath God said . . . ?" (Gen. 3:1). By the way, the Devil will put a question mark where God has put a period. God makes a statement, and the Devil comes along and questions that statement. Why is the world in trouble? We have listened to the Devil. When we allow him to put question marks where God put exclamation points, we suffer the consequences.

> **The Devil will put a question mark where God has put a period.**

Our country is suffering in the spiritual realm. Churches are suffering, families are suffering, individuals are suffering. Anytime we listen to the Devil, we turn a deaf ear to God. Anytime you face the Devil, your back is turned on God.

The Devil came along with his dirty deal and asked, "Did God really say?" Let us read verses 2–7 of Genesis 3:

"And the woman said unto the serpent, We may eat of the fruit of the trees of the garden:

"But of the fruit of the tree which is in the midst of the garden, God hath said, Ye shall not eat of it, neither shall ye touch it, lest ye die.

"And the serpent said unto the woman, Ye shall not surely die:

"For God doth know that in the day ye eat thereof, then your eyes shall be opened, and ye shall be as gods, knowing good and evil.

"And when the woman saw that the tree was good for food, and that it was pleasant to the eyes, and a tree to be desired to make one

wise, she took of the fruit thereof, and did eat, and gave also unto her husband with her; and he did eat.

"And the eyes of them both were opened, and they knew that they were naked."

A while ago Adam and Eve were naked and not ashamed; now they have disobeyed God, listened to Satan, and have become ashamed in the Garden. Shame came upon them in the early days of their existence. "And they heard the voice of the Lord God walking in the garden in the cool of the day: and Adam and his wife hid themselves" (Gen. 3:8). They were not hiding before. They were just as naked before, but there was no shame.

It is a shame that we listen to the Devil. The Devil will entice you and try to make you think premarital sex is not wrong. That is neither God's way nor God's will.

Satan will tell you there is no harm in doing anything you want to do if you go to church or if you do it in moderation. How many people would one have to kill to be called a murderer?

". . . and Adam and his wife hid themselves from the presence of the LORD God amongst the trees of the garden.

"And the LORD God called unto Adam, and said unto him, Where art thou?"—Gen. 3:8, 9.

God already knew where Adam was. God knows where you are! He is not trying to guess what pew you are sitting on, what your employment number is, your social security number, your area code, your house number, your telephone number. He knows all of that. But He asked Adam a direct question. He put Adam in a spot where he had to answer God.

God is going to put you and me in a spot where we have to answer Him.

". . . Where art thou?

"And he said, I heard thy voice in the garden, and I was afraid, because I was naked; and I hid myself.

"And he said, Who told thee that thou wast naked? Hast thou eaten of the tree, whereof I commanded thee that thou shouldest not eat?

"And the man said, The woman whom thou gavest to be with me, she gave me of the tree, and I did eat."—Gen. 3:9–12.

Passing the buck, Adam? Guys, why don't we quit blaming our wives? Why don't we share the blame too? Doesn't Adam sound so innocent? By the way, if the woman had said to Satan, "Talk to my husband about it," things might have turned out differently. When Satan said, "Now, did God say this? And don't you . . . ?" she ought to have said, "Wait just a minute, Mr. Devil. Wait until I get my husband, and you talk to him."

The man is the head of the home, the head of the household, or should be. Some men I know have spaghetti for a backbone, so they are not the heads of their homes.

"And the Lord God said unto the woman, What is this that thou hast done?" And the woman said, "The serpent beguiled me, and I did eat" (Gen. 3:13). How many times have you said, "The Devil made me do it"? You are passing the buck, blaming somebody else.

Look at verses 16–19:

"Unto the woman he said, I will greatly multiply thy sorrow and thy conception; in sorrow thou shalt bring forth children; and thy desire shall be to thy husband, and he shall rule over thee.

"And unto Adam he said, Because thou hast hearkened unto the voice of thy wife, and hast eaten of the tree, of which I commanded thee, saying, Thou shalt not eat of it: cursed is the ground for thy sake; in sorrow shalt thou eat of it all the days of thy life;

"Thorns also and thistles shall it bring forth to thee; and thou shalt eat the herb of the field;

"In the sweat of thy face shalt thou eat bread, till thou return unto the ground; for out of it wast thou taken: for dust thou art, and unto dust shalt thou return."

We see that the first family disobeyed the restrictions God imposed upon them. Anytime we disobey those restrictions, we have to suffer the consequences.

I see three consequences that came from the first family's disobeying God's restrictions.

Disobedience Results in Sorrow. "I will greatly multiply thy sorrow and thy conception; in sorrow thou shalt bring forth children" (Gen. 3:16). Mothers know exactly what that means.

Disobedience Results in Subjection. This is subjection of the wife to the husband. " . . . Thy desire shall be to thy husband." Wife, seek the best for your husband. Give him pleasure.

" . . . And he [your husband] shall rule over thee." The family chain of command is God in Heaven, the husband, the wife, and then the children. When it gets turned around, when the wife rules the roost, when the children are in the saddle, you have a perfect prescription for misery.

Someone said that everything in the modern home is operated by a switch except the children. What is wrong in America? Children having their way and rebelling against parental authority. If they get by with it in the home, they will try to get by with it at school and on the job. They think they can get by with it out in the world, but rebellion has to be subdued sooner or later. It is easier to subdue a one-year-old than a ten-year-old or an eighteen-year-old.

God did not take Eve out of Adam's head that he might be the lord over her. By the way, if husbands have to say every third day, "I am the head of this castle," chances are they are not. The man has authority over the household.

The wife's duty to her husband is stated in Ephesians 5:22: "Wives, submit yourselves unto your own husbands, as unto the Lord." You are thinking, *Well, my husband just won't take the lead.* Give him a chance. You have been leading him around so long that he has not had a chance to exercise any authority.

"For the husband is the head of the wife, even as Christ is the head of the church: and he is the saviour of the body.

"Therefore as the church is subject unto Christ, so let the wives be to their own husbands in every thing."—Eph. 5:23, 24.

Wives, does it say "in most things"? No! "In *every* thing."

Ephesians 5:25 contains just as strong a command regarding the husband's responsibility to his wife; it is just as inspired, just as infallible as the verses about wives. "Husbands, love your wives, even as Christ also loved the church, and gave himself for it."

When you and I love our wives as Jesus Christ loved the church, our wives will be in subjection to us. They will want to do what we want them to do if we come to the place in our relationship where we love them as much as Christ loved the church. Jesus loved the church enough to purchase it with His own blood. He died for it. The church, the local body of believers, is in absolute subjection to Jesus Christ.

Now watch the parallel. Even as God has set the husband to be the authority, the head, to lead, to guide in the home, to direct it, so God has set the pastor in the church to lead this body, to guide this body, to show pastoral authority to this body.

God in His Word also draws the parallel between Christ's relationship to His church and the husband's relationship to his wife. When a husband starts loving his wife enough to die for her, enough to lay down his life and shed his blood, we will have no problem with a wife's being in subjection to her husband. That is God's way, God's plan.

Disobedience Results in Sweat. Genesis 3:19 says: "In the sweat of thy face shalt thou eat bread." In other words, 'By the sweat of your brow you will earn your living.' Perhaps there never would have been perspiration had the first parents not sinned against God. Perhaps there would never have been that horror we have about work. One fellow said, "Work doesn't bother me. I treat it just like the mule; I pull away from it." Many people are like that. Many are scared to death of work. But God said that you have to work to live, to eat: "In the sweat of thy face [your brow]."

Sorrow, subjection and **sweat** are the consequences of the first family's disobeying the restrictions.

God's restrictions are relevant today. Moses lived and wrote about 1400 B.C. If what Moses wrote thirty-five hundred years ago was true for his time, then it is true now because God's Word does not change.

Exodus 20 lists some restrictions on every member of the family.

1. *"Thou shalt have no other gods before me."*
2. *"Thou shalt not make unto thee any graven image."*
3. *"Thou shalt not take the name of the LORD thy God in vain."*
4. *"Remember the sabbath day, to keep it holy."*
5. *"Honour thy father and thy mother: that thy days may be long upon the land which the LORD thy God giveth thee."*
6. *"Thou shalt not kill."*
7. *"Thou shalt not commit adultery."*
8. *"Thou shalt not steal."*
9. *"Thou shalt not bear false witness."* Do not tell a lie against your neighbor.
10. *"Thou shalt not covet thy neighbour's house, thou shalt not covet thy neighbour's wife, nor his manservant, nor his maidservant, nor his ox, nor his ass, nor any thing that is thy neighbour's."*

Right away you say, "Well, I've never killed anybody. I've never committed adultery."

Wait a minute! James 2:10 is a mind boggler, an earthshaker: "For whosoever shall keep the whole law, and yet offend in one point, he is guilty of all." In other words, God just throws the book at us. You say, "Well, I haven't been as bad as these other men I knew," or, "I haven't been as bad as she has been."

Wait a minute! Every one of us would be in Hell if we had what we deserve. Don't tell me how good you are. None of us is good. There is not a person who has not sinned against God, who has not broken a commandment of His, not one. If we have broken one, the Bible says we are guilty of all. May God help us to live in the fear of God.

THE FIRST FAMILY WAS STRUCK WITH TRAGEDY

The first family had two sons, Cain and Abel. They were brought into the world by the same parents. They ate the same food, wore the same type clothing, played the same games, received the same kind of education, were subjected to the same lifestyle, and received the same religious training. Yet they were altogether different. Abel's blood-sacrifice offering was accepted by God, while Cain's offering, the fruit of his own labor, was rejected. Thus, in a fit of anger Cain slew his brother Abel. Remember, the two were products of the same environment, yet they were diversified in character and different in temperament.

If you have two children, don't expect them to be alike. Many parents make the mistake of thinking that every one of their children is going to have the same temperament, to do the same thing in the same way, and react alike to every situation.

Parents, don't expect all of your children to act and react the same way. Although you give them the same teaching, training, food, clothes, school and the same church, be aware that they are different.

The consequence of jealousy in the first family was murder. The consequence of the murder is in Genesis 4:11, 12:

"And now art thou cursed from the earth . . . When thou tillest the ground, it shall not henceforth yield unto thee her strength; a fugitive and a vagabond shalt thou be in the earth."

I conclude by saying three things:
- God ordained the family.

• God operates within the family.
• God offers guidelines for the family.

DEALING WITH THE DEVIL

The best way for your family to deal with the Devil is NOT to make a deal with him.

You can win the victory through Christ as you:

> **The best way for your family to deal with the Devil is NOT to make a deal with him.**

1. "Resist the devil" in the power of the Holy Spirit (Jas. 4:7; I Pet. 5:8,9).
2. Do not give the Devil any room to operate in your family (Eph. 4:27).
3. Attack the Devil with the Word of God (Matt. 4:4).
4. The Devil is an ACCUSER—he will accuse your family to God.
5. The Devil is a SLANDERER—he will slander your family.
6. The Devil is a DESTROYER—he will attempt to destroy your family.
7. The Devil is a LIAR—he will lie to your family.
8. The Devil is a DECEIVER—he will deceive your family.

Thank God, the Devil is a defeated enemy, and Jesus Christ will destroy his works (I John 3:8).

THE FAMILY THAT FOUND GRACE

—NOAH—
Genesis 6:5–22

"And GOD saw that the wickedness of man was great in the earth, and that every imagination of the thoughts of his heart was only evil continually.

"And it repented the LORD that he had made man on the earth, and it grieved him at his heart.

"And the LORD said, I will destroy man whom I have created from the face of the earth; both man, and beast, and the creeping thing, and the fowls of the air; for it repenteth me that I have made them.

"But Noah found grace in the eyes of the LORD.

"These are the generations of Noah: Noah was a just man and perfect in his generations, and Noah walked with God.

"And Noah begat three sons, Shem, Ham, and Japheth.

"The earth also was corrupt before God, and the earth was filled with violence.

"And God looked upon the earth, and, behold, it was corrupt; for all flesh had corrupted his way upon the earth.

"And God said unto Noah, The end of all flesh is come before me; for the earth is filled with violence through them; and, behold, I will destroy them with the earth.

"Make thee an ark of gopher wood; rooms shalt thou make in the ark, and shalt pitch it within and without with pitch.

"And this is the fashion which thou shalt make it of: The length of the ark shall be three hundred cubits, the breadth of it fifty cubits, and the height of it thirty cubits.

"A window shalt thou make to the ark, and in a cubit shalt thou *finish it above; and the door of the ark shalt thou set in the side thereof; with lower, second, and third stories shalt thou make it.*

"And, behold, I, even I, do bring a flood of waters upon the earth, to destroy all flesh, wherein is the breath of life, from under heaven; and every thing that is in the earth shall die.

"But with thee will I establish my covenant; and thou shalt come into the ark, thou, and thy sons, and thy wife, and thy sons' wives with thee.

"And of every living thing of all flesh, two of every sort shalt thou bring into the ark, to keep them alive with thee; they shall be male and female.

"Of fowls after their kind, and of cattle after their kind, of every creeping thing of the earth after his kind, two of every sort shall come unto thee, to keep them alive.

"And take thou unto thee of all food that is eaten, and thou shalt gather it to thee; and it shall be for food for thee, and for them.

"Thus did Noah; according to all that God commanded him, so did he."

An unusual story of an unusual family. God is interested in your family. He knows all the fears that your family has, all the problems that you face. He knows the decisions that you have to make about your employment, about the place you are living, about the car you are driving, about your friends. God knows all about these things. What concerns you as a family concerns God. He is vitally interested in your family.

> **God is interested in your family.**

I will point out four reasons why I feel Noah's family was able to survive the storm. Apply these things to your own life.

I am aware that Noah lived thousands of years ago. I am aware that this culture is different, civilizations have come and gone, cultures have risen and fallen; fads and fashions, men and machines have changed the way we live. But one thing is exactly as it was in Noah's day—the heart of mankind. Hearts are the same. I know God wants your head, but if God gets your heart, He has all of you. It all begins with the heart.

NOAH'S FAMILY SURVIVED IN A WORLD OF SIN AND DEGRADATION

We can identify with that. Remember what Jesus said, "And as it was in the days of Noe [Noah], so shall it be also in the days of the Son of man." Many of the things that were happening in Noah's world are happening in our world. Conditions made it difficult for Noah to bring up a family in righteousness, morality, honesty and purity. Conditions make it difficult in our world, but it can be done. The Bible says that the wickedness of man was very great over all the earth. We are talking about the whole human race. No wonder the Scriptures in Romans 3:10,12 say, "There is none righteous, no, not one"; 'there is none that doeth good.' Man by nature is a sinner, a rebel against God. Man by nature runs from the restrictions that God puts on him.

The whole earth of Noah's day was filled with men of rebellion, men who were obstinate, arrogant, sinful, depraved, iniquitous, full of lusts, and full of selfishness. The totality of every man was evil. God has twenty-twenty vision; He is a fair referee. He calls them just as He sees them. Look again at Genesis 6:5: "GOD saw that the wickedness of man was great in the earth, and that every imagination of the thoughts of his heart [not

19

just every imagination of the heart but every imagination of the thoughts of his heart] was only evil continually."

The men of Noah's day were totally depraved. Every imagination was an evil imagination. Every thought was evil; every ambition was sensual; every purpose was devilish; every desire was licentious. It was a heart matter, and that is where the trouble lies. We sing that song, "Is your heart right with God?" Jesus, the greatest Authority, gives us a commentary on it in the Gospel according to Mark: "For from within, out of the heart of men, proceed evil thoughts, adulteries, fornications, murders, thefts, covetousness, wickedness, deceit, lasciviousness, an evil eye, blasphemy, pride, foolishness: All these evil things come from within, and defile the man" (7:21).

How is your heart? Is it right with God? Do you have a love for Jesus Christ? Have you given just a mental assent to the fact that there is a Christ, a Saviour? Or do you really know Him in your heart? Do you love Him in your heart? How is your heart toward your husband, your wife, your children, your neighbor, your fellow Christian? It is a heart matter. "God saw that . . . every imagination of the thoughts of [man's] heart was only evil continually."

The world conditions of the twentieth century make it very difficult to rear children. The crime rate is at an all-time high. A major crime is committed every five seconds in America. There is violence such as we have never seen before. The drug culture baffles the mind. There are eleven million alcoholics. A hundred thousand people die every year because of some alcohol-related accident. In my opinion, alcohol is about the worst drug we have in the world, and we put the least amount of emphasis on doing anything about it. Cocaine kills seven thousand a year, but alcohol kills a hundred thousand and injures five hundred forty thousand. Illicit sex, promiscuity and homosexuality characterize the day in which we live. Surely the coming of Christ will be soon.

Everywhere preachers are preaching on the second coming. Oh, I know you say, "Just like it says in the Scripture, 'Since the fathers fell asleep, all things continue as they were from the beginning of the creation.' All we have heard is the coming of Christ, the end of the world."

Wait a moment! Peter says, "One day is with the Lord as a thousand years, and a thousand years as one day" (II Pet. 3:8). Do you know what that means? Jesus has only been back in Heaven for two days. Some wonderful things have happened on the third day. His coming draweth nigh.

The world has gone mad with sin, violence, crime, drugs and everything else. Jesus parallels this day with Noah's day, and He says the days are just alike. Thank God, we have a great child-rearing manual—the Holy Bible. It is difficult to bring up children in the fear and admonition of the Lord when they are being brainwashed in school, in the community, and by television. But it **can be done**, and it **must be done**. If this generation is lost, the world is lost. If this generation is not saved, the next generation will not have a chance to be saved. When He put these principles in His Book, God knew they were eternal, that they would never grow old, would never be refuted. They remain the same. The Bible is better than any and all of the child psychology books that have been printed. These eternal principles in the Bible have been tried and proven. For instance, "Train up a child in the way he should go: and when he is old, he will not depart from it" (Prov. 22:6).

Someone may say he knows a lot of exceptions. Now

wait! Does the one making that statement really know what it means to train up children? It is more than bringing them to Sunday school. Many parents think they can bring their children to Sunday school, turn them over to the teacher and the pastor, and everything will be all right. It is not going to be all right! If they do not get training at Mother's knee and by Father's hand, they won't get it in church. Training them up in the way of the Lord is more than bringing them to Sunday school or to church on Sunday night or Wednesday night. **Training** has to begin in the **home**. That is a tried and true principle.

> **Training has to begin in the home.**

Rules and regulations in the Word of God? Yes. Basic values of morality, honesty, purity, correction and discipline. Proverbs 13:24 declares, "He that spareth his rod hateth his son: but he that loveth him chasteneth him betimes." *Betimes* means "often." Not once a year, but **often** chasten, discipline, regulate, govern.

Parents, children expect discipline, and they want discipline. Many a young man out there is wondering, *Why didn't Dad tell me what to do? Why didn't Dad tell me this was wrong?* Children need it, expect it and deserve it. God has outlined it in His Book.

Noah's family survived even though they lived in a world of sin and degradation. Your family can also survive if you bring them up in the fear and admonition of the Lord. That does not mean you will be problem-free. God never said that. In Genesis, chapter 4, we see two boys who were raised in the same home, ate the same food, wore the same kind of clothes, had the same kind of training—two boys who did everything basically the same. One turned out to be a murderer.

NOAH'S FAMILY REFUSED TO BE LIKE THE WORLD

We are **in** the world but not **of** the world. Genesis 6:5 tells us how wicked, evil and sinful the world was. Then verse 8 states, "But Noah . . . ." The world was wicked, vile, sinful and degrading in every sense of each word, "**But** Noah found grace in the eyes of the LORD."

Here was a morning star in a dark sky. Here was a man who was different. When Noah was building that ark, they laughed at him and scorned him. They must have chided, "You idiot! You fool! It has never rained. What are you doing building a boat?" Noah would have answered them, "Because God said to build an ark."

Some of the people in your neighborhood, some of the people you work with are laughing. They think it is stupid for you to come to church and put your tithes and offerings in the collection plate. But you and I are on a different economy. The Book says, "But seek ye first the kingdom of God, and his righteousness; and all these things shall be added unto you."

We are going by the Book. It is in the Book. You and I can have discipline even in the midst of a sinful, chaotic, violent, sexual, mad, materialistic, mixed-up world; we can survive if we refuse to be like the world.

Noah, the father in this home, found grace. It all starts with Daddy. Daddy, when your children are small you may not think they will ever go

> **It all starts with the father.**

astray, but you just wait until they get a bit older. I have heard men say about their three-year-old daughters, "My daughter never will do that." It is one thing when they are three; it is another thing when they are thirteen. Put in them now some principles that will last.

Some things must be accomplished at home. Don't expect the pastor or the Sunday school teacher to raise them for you in the midst of a perverse generation. As the head of the home, God is depending on you, Daddy, to lead your family to Sunday school, church, soul winning, reading the Bible, prayer, and righteous living. Don't try to warn your son of the dangers of cocaine while you sip your beer. Mother, don't try to teach your daughter decency in dress while you are exposing your body through indecent attire. Double standards won't work.

We read in I Timothy 2:9, "In like manner also [I will], that women adorn themselves in modest apparel." No one need tell you that you women are wearing your dresses too short, or tell you that you ought not to wear shorts. You know that without having to be told. You know what decent dress is all about. You are not dumb. You know what God's Word says. You know the difference between modest and immodest. Set a good example.

Verse 8 of chapter 6 says, "But Noah found grace in the eyes of the LORD." In verse 9 we read that Noah was a just man, that his behavior toward God and man was honorable, and that he was mature.

Parents, submit yourselves to God, and He will give you **wisdom** and **understanding** of His Word; God will give you **counsel**; He will give you **insight** and **foresight**. I would highly recommend that every family read a chapter in the book of Proverbs, God's wisdom book, every day to get wisdom. In it God addresses sons, daughters, fathers, mothers and families. He addresses our every need in Proverbs. Ephesians 6:4 exhorts us, "And, ye fathers, provoke not your children to wrath: but bring them up [rear them] in the nurture and admonition of the Lord."

Noah's family was able to survive the Flood because they refused to be like the world.

WHAT IS THE CHRISTIAN'S RELA- TIONSHIP TO THE WORLD?

Christians should not love the world.

"Love not the world, neither the things that are in the world. If any man love the world, the love of the Father is not in him.

"For all that is in the world, the lust of the flesh, and the lust of the eyes, and the pride of life, is not of the Father, but is of the world.

"And the world passeth away, and the lust thereof: but he that doeth the will of God abideth for ever." —I John 2:15–17.

Christians should not be conformed to this world's system. The easiest thing in all the world is to flow with the tide. Anybody can float downstream. It takes a real man, a real woman to go against the tide, against the wave of popular opinion. Young people, if your peers say, "Come on, let's have a beer," you say, "No, thank you. I don't drink beer." If you are invited, "Come on, let's blow a cigarette," you answer, "I don't smoke." Thousands upon thousands who will smoke their first cigarette today, will die sooner or later because of it. It won't get you this week, but it will eventually!

When they say, "Let's go steal a car," you answer back, "I don't steal. I don't cheat. I don't lie. I'm a Christian." If you can say "No!" the first time, the second time will be easier. Separate yourself from the world.

Paul said in Romans 12:1, "I beseech you therefore, brethren, by the mercies of God, that ye present your bodies a living sacrifice, holy, acceptable unto God, which is your reasonable service." God does not demand anything unreasonable. It is our reasonable service that we **surrender** ourselves, **dedicate** ourselves and **commit** ourselves to Him. Be not conformed to this world's system. Don't be like the world, don't walk like the world, don't dress like the world, don't smell like the world, don't look like the world, and don't think like the world. If we belong to Christ, the world has every right to expect us to be something different.

God does not want spiritual nuts. He wants fruit-bearing Christians. Every man, woman, boy and girl has enough intelligence to say, "This is the way I am going to live my life. This is how I will treat my family. This is how I will act toward others. This is what I am not going to do."

Daniel could handle lions at age ninety because he learned to handle temptation at nineteen. When they put the king's dish before him, he said, "No." When they put the king's wine before him, he said, "No." You had better say it the first time and make your stand absolute, certain, clear and sure so no one will have to wonder where you stand. "And be not conformed to this world: but be ye transformed by the renewing of your mind" (Rom. 12:2).

Christians should not be overcome by the world. Don't be in love with it, conformed to it, or overcome by it. Jesus said in John 16:33, "In the world ye shall have tribulation [trials, problems, difficulties, heartaches]: but be of good cheer; I have overcome the world."

Follow this logic. As a saved person, are you not in Christ? If He has overcome the world, you too can overcome the world because you are in Him. This is the way it works: we are in Him, He is in us, and since He has already overcome the world, so have we.

Do not be in love with, conformed to, or overcome by the world. Noah's family survived the storm because they refused to be like the world.

NOAH'S FAMILY COOPERATED IN FAMILY TOGETHERNESS

It is sad that now we have no time when families can sit down together. If we do, we are so busy watching each other's favorite television program that we don't talk. When was the last time you got your family together and said, "Let's cut off television and play jacks, bounce a ball, or do something together"? When did you last sit down and laugh at each other, talk to each other, or eat a bowl of popcorn together? When have you just sat down and fellowshiped together in the home? We don't have time for any of that anymore. We are zip, zap, going and coming, coming and going. We have so many irons in the fire that we are all burned out. We'd better take time just to sit down and enjoy each other. Noah's family survived because they cooperated in building and maintaining family togetherness.

Family togetherness starts with Daddy. Daddy, it is not your wife's responsibility; it is

> **Family togetherness starts with Daddy.**

yours. Does verse 22 say, "Thus did Mrs. Noah"? Of course not. "Thus did Noah; according to all that God commanded him, so did he." It begins with the head of the home. It begins with obedience, just doing what God said do. He provides the grace. They worked **together** building and maintaining family togetherness.

They went into the ark together. "And Noah went in, and his sons, and his wife, and his sons' wives with him, into the ark, because of the waters of the flood" (Gen. 7:7). Isn't it beautiful to see families **together** in worship! Once there were family pews in churches where the whole family sat **together**. They went into the ark as a family unit. Isn't it a beautiful thing to see families come into church **together**! They went into the ark **together**. They worshiped **together**.

They exited the ark together. "And Noah went forth, and his sons, and his wife, and his sons' wives with him" (Gen. 8:18).

They erected the altar together. "And Noah builded an altar unto the LORD; and took of every clean beast" (Gen. 8:20). It goes without saying, it is unwritten, but Noah's family was there when he built the altar and got his family **together** for prayer and sacrifice.

They enjoyed God's blessings together. "And God blessed Noah and his sons" (Gen. 9:1), that is, his family. God blesses family togetherness. Families should not only **pray** together; they should **play** together so they can **stay** together.

Daddy, if you do not pray and play with your children today, you will find them alienated from you tomorrow, and you will wonder, *What on earth happened? I gave him a car; I let him do what he wanted to do; I gave him spending money; I bought his clothes, and now he is gone.* But have you **played** with him? Have you **prayed** with him? Have you **stayed** with him? It takes more than buying him a car, more than buying him a suit of clothes or sending him a ticket to the Super Bowl. It is better to pray with them when they are at home than it is to pray for them after they are gone. Ephesians 6:4 is explicit: "Fathers . . . bring them . . . up." Paul didn't say when they got to be eighteen that you are to get concerned about them.

Rather, he said to "bring them up in the nurture and admonition of the Lord."

Mother, teach your girls to cook, to sew, to clean house (that is, if you yourself have learned to do those things!). Let them burn a little boiling water sometimes! It won't hurt. Teach them how to do the basic things. God said in I Timothy 5:14, "I will therefore that the younger women marry, bear children, guide the house." I didn't make that up. Dr. Spock didn't write that. Your child psychologist didn't write that. God said to teach them how to live and love, how to cook and wash dishes, how to clean house and sew.

Noah's family survived because there was a family **togetherness**.

NOAH'S FAMILY FOUND REFUGE IN THE ARK

The rains fell, the fountains of the deep were broken up, the waters rose, and Noah and his family went into the ark as God had commanded: "Come thou and all thy house into the ark." God does not require **sinless perfection**, but He does demand **personal righteousness**. God requires parents to set a proper example before their children.

Parents, here are three principles that will help you:

1. **God requires obedience.** "Thus did Noah; according to all that God commanded him, so did he" (Gen. 6:22). "And God blessed Noah and his sons" (Gen. 9:1). So be obedient.

2. **God remembers the family that trusts in Him.** "God remembered Noah" (Gen. 8:1). God remembers those who trust in Him.

3. God rejoices when families worship Him at an altar of prayer.

"And Noah builded an altar unto the Lord; and took of every clean beast, and of every clean fowl, and offered burnt offerings on the altar.

"And the Lord smelled a sweet savour; and the Lord said in his heart, I will not again curse the ground any more for man's sake."—Gen. 8:20, 21.

He wanted to preserve every family; He wanted every family to build an altar and to worship Him. God rejoices to see the family together at the altar.

God wants you to survive the storm that is threatening your family. If it is a storm of temptation, materialism or neglect; if it is a storm of carelessness—whatever it may be, God wants your family to survive the storm. God has proven His concern in the Person of His Son, Jesus Christ, in the power of the Holy Spirit, and in the writing of His Word. God has already proven to you that He wants you to survive the storm. He has raised an umbrella of protection over your family. Remember, He built a hedge around Job, and God has done the same thing for you!

GOD'S SURVIVAL KIT FOR THE FAMILY

1. ENTER the ark of safety in Jesus Christ. No family can survive without Jesus Christ.
2. MAINTAIN a family altar of daily devotions. No family can survive without prayer.
3. OPERATE your home by biblical principles. No family can survive without the Bible.

4. SEPARATE yourselves from the evils of this world's system. No family can survive without godly living.

5. COOPERATE in building family togetherness. No family can survive without the spirit of unity.

THE FAMILY THAT BLESSED THE WORLD

—ABRAHAM—
Genesis 12:1–5

"Now the Lord had said unto Abram, Get thee out of thy country, and from thy kindred, and from thy father's house, unto a land that I will shew thee:

"And I will make of thee a great nation, and I will bless thee, and make thy name great; and thou shalt be a blessing:

"And I will bless them that bless thee, and curse him that curseth thee: and in thee shall all families of the earth be blessed.

"So Abram departed, as the Lord had spoken unto him; and Lot went with him: and Abram was seventy and five years old when he departed out of Haran.

"And Abram took Sarai his wife, and Lot his brother's son, and all their substance that they had gathered, and the souls that they had gotten in Haran; and they went forth to go into the land of Canaan; and into the land of Canaan they came."

The family of Abraham is one of the most prominent in all the Old Testament. In fact, it is one of the most prominent families in the entire Word of God.

God used Abraham's family as an example for all the families of the earth. Observe what God said to Abraham: "In thee shall all families of the earth be blessed."

I believe God wants to use your family and mine as examples to other families. When you get into your automobile and drive to church, you say to your neighbors and the entire community, "I believe in the church. I believe in the family going to church together." When they see your family get in the car, all dressed up and going to church, they see before them a good example. But that is only the beginning of the example that God wants us to set before others.

God used Abraham's family to establish some principles that continue throughout the revelation of God's Word. These principles are just as appropriate for our families in the twentieth century as they were for Abraham's family in his day. You see, methods are many, but principles are few. Methods change often; principles never do. The four thousand years since Abraham lived have not made one iota of difference in the basic principles of truth, righteousness, holiness, purity, morality, family values and basic truth. You and I need them as much as Abraham needed them—actually, more than Abraham needed them then. These principles in the family of Abraham occupy a permanent place in the plan, program and purpose of God for the whole human race.

Look at the last part of verse 3: ". . . and in thee shall all families of the earth be blessed." Abraham's family can be described as the family that enjoyed the blessings of God. In verse 2, God said, "I will bless thee." In verse 3, God said, "And I will bless them that bless thee, and curse him that curseth thee." Now look at verse 2 in chapter 13: "And Abram was very rich in cattle, in silver, and in gold." There is nothing wrong with a family's being wealthy. God wants us to enjoy peace, prosperity, plenty and productivity. He wants the very best for His children.

Mother, Father, do you not want the best for your children? Don't you believe that God our Father wants the very best for us? We read in Psalm 84:11, ". . . no good thing will he withhold from them that walk uprightly." It is God's design, God's desire, God's determination that His people be blessed. Certainly there is no wrong, no harm in enjoying your money. If you have money, then praise God for it; but if money has you, ask God to take money away from you or to take you away from money. Money is a wonderful servant but a terrible master. God wants all to enjoy the good things of life.

God wants us all to be happy. God wants us all to be free. God wants us all to enjoy life. God wants us all to be prosperous and have the things that will bring happiness to us as long as we know how to use prosperity.

The family of Abraham was blessed of God. I will share three reasons why God blessed Abraham's family.

ABRAHAM MAINTAINED A RIGHT RELATIONSHIP WITH GOD

There were some flaws in Abraham's family, some problems, some sins. There were sins in Abraham's life; he was not perfect, but he did maintain a right relationship with God. This relationship is seen in the fact that Abraham built an **altar** everywhere he went. He believed in **worship**. He believed in **prayer**. He believed in **sacrifice**. He believed in **giving**. He believed in the **truth**. He believed in **holiness** and **righteousness**. Abraham believed God.

First, Abraham built an altar at Sichem, the very first stop in the land of Canaan. He didn't wait until he picked out four or five different places to live. He did not wait until he changed his residence a dozen times. As soon as he got into the land of Canaan he built an altar. Look at verses 6 and 7 in this 12th chapter. The last part of

verse 5 says that "into the land of Canaan they came."
Now verses 6 and 7:

*"And Abram passed through the land unto the place of Sichem,
unto the plain of Moreh. And the Canaanite was then in the land.*
*"And the LORD appeared unto Abram, and said, Unto thy seed
will I give this land: and there* [at Sichem, the first stop] *builded
he an altar unto the LORD, who appeared unto him."*

Abraham was a man of the altar.

> **The father must be a
> man of the altar.**

Dad, you had better be a
man of the altar. You should
lead in family devotions. You
say, "I am embarrassed." Then
get over your embarrassment. You are not embarrassed to
talk to them about the baseball team, the stock market, or
about your job. So don't be embarrassed to talk to your
family about God, righteousness, truth, sobriety, honesty.
Lead them to an altar, pray **with** them and **for** them.

Abraham built an altar as soon as he arrived in
Canaan. Your priority should be to establish a church
home and a family altar as soon as you locate in a city. I
don't even see where Abraham found a house first. He
certainly didn't find a job first. He first built an altar giving priority to the main thing. The first thing that he did
in the first place where he stopped was to build an altar
unto God.

Let me give you a warning: Don't locate in a city
where there is not a good, Bible-believing, fundamental,
independent Baptist church where you can worship
God. You would be better off to stay where you are and
make less money than to go to another city that doesn't
have a testimony for God and where you can make more
money. Money is not everything. Find a church home

and build a family altar immediately. Give it priority, as Abraham did.

Genesis 12:8 tells us Abraham built an altar when he moved from Sichem to Bethel: "And he removed from thence unto a mountain on the east of Beth-el, and pitched his tent, having Beth-el on the west, and Hai on the east: and there he builded an altar unto the LORD, and called upon the name of the Lord."

He stayed at Sichem awhile, moved over to Bethel, built another altar, and called upon the name of the Lord. *Bethel* means "house of God."

Now follow this. Here was Bethel, and here was Hai. *Bethel* means "the house of God," and *Hai* means "the place of ruin." Here we are at the house of God, Bethel; here is the place of ruin, Hai; and in between is the altar of prayer.

What am I saying? The only thing between you and absolute ruin is the altar of prayer, worship and sacrifice. The altar that you build to God is the only thing standing between you and the place of ruin for your family. So build one and maintain it.

Abraham lived near the house of God. Abraham recognized the importance of prayer. The last part of verse 8 says he "called upon the name of the LORD."

Prayer is important. That does not mean you must spend two hours every day with your family in prayer. You probably do not have that much time. But where is there a person who couldn't spend a couple of minutes in prayer with his family? Prayer changes things, circumstances and people.

Aren't you glad God said, "Call unto me, and I will answer thee, and shew thee great and mighty things, which thou knowest not"? Prayer is the key that unlocks the storehouse of God. Matthew 18:19 follows through on what Abraham was doing—building an altar and praying. Jesus promised, "That if two of you shall agree on earth as touching any thing that they shall ask, it shall be done for them of my Father which is in heaven." Jesus is as good as His word.

Abraham built an altar at Sichem. Then when he moved to Bethel, he built another altar.

Then a famine came to the land of Canaan, and Abraham journeyed down to Egypt. Look at verse 10 in chapter 12: "And there was a famine in the land: and Abram went down into Egypt to sojourn there." He left Bethel, the house of God, and went down to Egypt. Any direction away from the house of God is down. Anytime we leave the house of God we are going down, down, down. Abraham left the house of God. He didn't depend upon God. As soon as the famine struck, he thought he had to go where there was food. He should have waited on God, who has control of all the food, all the riches of Heaven and earth. Abraham went down to Egypt, and he had a lapse of faith down there.

Look at verse 11. Abraham started lying before he ever got into Egypt. "And it came to pass, when he was come near to enter into Egypt, that he said unto Sarai his wife, Behold now, I know that thou art a fair woman [a beautiful woman] to look upon."

In other words, 'Sarai, when they see you, they are going to demand you. So when we get there, tell them that you are my sister.' He started lying before he ever got to Egypt (the world). You don't have to go down into Egypt to start sinning against God. The moment you leave the house of God trouble begins.

It is dangerous for people to miss church services. The Devil gains and you lose every time you miss a church service.

There is no evidence that Abraham worshiped at an altar as long as he was in Egypt. Out there in the world, away from God, away from the church, there is no place of prayer, no altar, no sacrifice, no worship.

But when Abraham got right with God and returned to the land of Canaan, he went right back to Bethel, right where he had started, and right back to the altar that he had left.

Now look at chapter 13, verses 1–4:

"And Abram went up out of Egypt, he, and his wife, and all that he had, and Lot with him, into the south.

"And Abram was very rich in cattle, in silver, and in gold.

"And he went on his journeys from the south even to Beth-el, unto the place where his tent had been at the beginning [close to the house of God], *between Beth-el and Hai;*

"Unto the place of the altar [he came out of Egypt, right back to the house of God, right back to the place of prayer], *which he had made there at the first: and there Abram called on the name of the Lord."*

When he got back out of Egypt, he went first to the house of God and the altar of prayer.

What a lesson for us! As long as they stayed close to the altar of prayer, Abraham's family was blessed because they maintained the proper relationship to God.

Is your family maintaining a good relationship with God? Are you on speaking terms with God? When was the last time you really had a heart-to-heart talk with God?

Maintaining a good relationship is why God blessed Abraham.

ABRAHAM MAINTAINED A SPIRIT OF GENEROSITY

> The curse of this age is selfishness.

The curse of this age is selfishness. History records that every war ever fought has been fought because of selfishness. Every home that has ever been broken up was broken up because of selfishness. Every problem, every burden, every difficulty in this world can be traced to somebody's selfishness. If it is a domestic problem, an economic problem, a social problem, a church problem, a family problem, a home problem—whatever the problem, every problem can be traced to selfishness.

If Christianity is anything, it is unselfishness. "For God so loved the world, that he gave" His life for us. Christianity is about giving.

> "What, giving again?" I ask in dismay.
> "Must I keep on giving and giving alway?"
> "Oh, no," said the angel, piercing me through.
> "Just keep giving 'til He stops giving to you."

When God stops, you can stop. But you had better not stop before then. You had better practice generosity.

Abraham was very generous in two areas. First, he was unselfish toward God in his stewardship of his tithes and offerings. Genesis 14:18–20 says:

"And Melchizedek king of Salem brought forth bread and wine: and he was the priest of the most high God.
"And he blessed him, and said, Blessed be Abram of the most

high God, possessor of heaven and earth:

"And blessed be the most high God, which hath delivered thine enemies into thy hand. And he [Abraham] *gave him* [Melchizedek, a type of Christ] *tithes of all."*

God will not bless a selfish person. God does bless unselfishness. Jesus said, "Give, and it shall be given unto you." If you are financially strapped, there is one of two things wrong: Either Jesus did not mean what He said, or there is something wrong in your giving program. 'Bring ye all the tithes into the storehouse, and see if I'll not open the windows of Heaven and pour out the blessings of God upon you.' Try it and see. God wants us to be generous.

Second, not only was Abraham generous toward God, but he was generous toward others. Our giving does not stop with giving to God. It includes others too. In chapter 18, verses 4–8, Abraham said:

"Let a little water, I pray you, be fetched, and wash your feet, and rest yourselves under the tree:

"And I will fetch a morsel of bread, and comfort ye your hearts; after that ye shall pass on . . . .

"And Abraham hastened into the tent unto Sarah, and said, Make ready quickly three measures of fine meal, knead it, and make cakes upon the hearth.

"And Abraham ran unto the herd, and fetcht a calf [not a tough old calf, too tough to eat but] *tender and good, and gave it unto a young man; and he hasted to dress it.*

"And he took butter, and milk, and the calf which he had dressed, and set it before them; and he stood by them under the tree, and they did eat."

Abraham was unselfish with others.

How is your record of generosity? When was the last time you gave a bit of money to somebody in need? You say, "I don't have it to spare." That is why you don't have it to spare. God said, 'If you give it, it will come back a hundredfold.'

Be generous. Teach your children to be unselfish (you don't have to teach them to be selfish; they already have that trait). Teach them to be generous, to be unselfish, to divide their candy, to share their toys, to play with others. Teach them to be unselfish, and they will grow up to be unselfish. Let them be selfish, and they will grow up to be selfish. Let them hear you criticize the church, and they will criticize the church. Let them hear you talk about the neighbors, and they will talk about the neighbors. Be a good example before them by your unselfishness and by your generosity.

God blessed Abraham's family because he maintained a spirit of generosity.

ABRAHAM MAINTAINED A DISCIPLINED HOUSEHOLD

"And the LORD said, Shall I hide from Abraham that thing which I do [destroy the cities of Sodom and Gomorrah, cities of homosexuality]*;*

"Seeing that Abraham shall surely become a great and mighty nation, and all the nations of the earth shall be blessed in him?

"For I know him [Abraham], *that he will command his children and his household* [not just the children, but the whole household] *after him, and they shall keep the way of the LORD, to do justice and judgment; that the LORD may bring upon Abraham that which he hath spoken of him."*—Gen. 18:17–19.

God could not bless Abraham unless he maintained a disciplined household. God will not bless us unless we maintain a disciplined household.

Notice God's assessment of Abraham in verse 19: "For I know him." God is saying, "I know Abraham. I know his **heart**, how he **feels**. I know Abraham's **head**, I know what he **thinks**. I know Abraham's **home**, how he **acts**."

God knows you and me. If God judged us according to our iniquities, none of us would be saved. If God started marking iniquities, none of us would be able to stand. But the grace of God, the mercy of God, the kindness of God, the compassion of God, the love of God are sufficient to cover all of our sins. God knows how we **feel**, how we **think**, how we **act**, how we **react**.

God said, "I know Abraham will discipline his children."

God said, "I know Abraham will be the head of his home."

God said, "I know Abraham will lead his family in the right way."

God said, "I know Abraham will do what is just and right in his home and by his family."

Just as God knew everything about Abraham, He knows everything about you and me. He knows our feelings, thoughts, motives, intentions, desires, purposes, aims, aspirations and goals. Bless God, He loves us in spite of all our sins and failures! God uses us in spite of what He knows about us. We're all guilty sinners before God. Only His mercy and grace have brought us to where we are. If we got what we deserved, every one of us would be in Hell. But God is rich in mercy.

Observe three things to be done in every home:

1. **Establish** God's **way**.

2. **Exercise** God's **wisdom** in managing your family.

3. **Exemplify** God's **will.**

Abraham was not perfect, but he set a good example. The key word is **example.** Are you setting the right kind of example in your home? Whatever Abraham did, he did by **faith.** Read the description of his faith in Hebrews 11. He left his homeland, a pagan land, and went over into the Promised Land by **faith.** He built altars by **faith.** He traveled by **faith.** He lived in tents and tabernacles by **faith.** By **faith** he looked for a city whose builder and maker is God.

If you've missed everything else, please don't miss this. God's blessings fell upon Abraham and his family because:

1. He was faithful in operating his home by divine principles;

2. He used wisdom in creating an atmosphere for godly living in his home.

Every parent, every child, every young person has that responsibility. The Bible is explicit: "Honour thy father and thy mother." Mother and Dad, if you want the right things, you had best put the right things into the home. Children, young people, you are a part of the home, a part of the family. Work together, establish principles, seek the wisdom of God, the will of God, the way of God in your home, in your life, in your studies—in everything. Our families need the same **priorities,** the same **patterns,** the same **principles** that Abraham's family needed.

We are not going to get them out of a child psychology book nor out of the latest "How to" book off the press. We get them while on our face before God at an altar of prayer.

I appeal to your better judgment to give God a chance at an altar of prayer to reinforce the divine principles by which you can govern your family and operate your home. That is the only hope of America. Will you let God bless your family? You hold the key.

THE FAMILY THAT BACKSLID

—LOT—
Genesis 13:5–13

"And Lot also, which went with Abram, had flocks, and herds, and tents.

"And the land was not able to bear them, that they might dwell together: for their substance was great, so that they could not dwell together.

"And there was a strife between the herdmen of Abram's cattle and the herdmen of Lot's cattle: and the Canaanite and the Perizzite dwelled then in the land.

"And Abram said unto Lot, Let there be no strife, I pray thee, between me and thee, and between my herdmen and thy herdmen; for we be brethren.

"Is not the whole land before thee? separate thyself, I pray thee, from me: if thou wilt take the left hand, then I will go to the right; or if thou depart to the right hand, then I will go to the left.

*"And Lot lifted up his eyes, and beheld all the plain of Jordan, that it was well watered every where, before the L*ORD *destroyed Sodom and Gomorrah, even as the garden of the L*ORD, *like the land of Egypt, as thou comest unto Zoar.*

"Then Lot chose him all the plain of Jordan; and Lot journeyed east: and they separated themselves the one from the other.

"Abram dwelled in the land of Canaan, and Lot dwelled in the cities of the plain, and pitched his tent toward Sodom.

*"But the men of Sodom were wicked and sinners before the L*ORD *exceedingly."*

This is the introduction to a sad, sad story—the story

of a family who had every chance to go the right way and do the right thing, but they chose the wrong way and ultimately did the wrong thing. This is the story of a family that moved from gloryland to ghoulishland. This is a story of a family whose "want" power was stronger than their "will" power.

Lot's family could be described as the family that *backslid.*

How tragic that many families are slipping away from the moorings, from the anchor, from Christ, from the church, from Christian principles, from God, from the Bible. Lot and his family had everything going for them, but they blew it. The calm turned to chaos. Lot found himself in a helpless position. The family's calmness turned into a chaotic experience when the head of that family, the father, the husband of that home, made the wrong choice. One simple decision didn't really seem at the time to have such grave consequences.

Often we say, "Well, I'll do this," and we make our plans. If we talk to God at all about them, it is after we have already made up our minds, and oftentimes that is too late. When our plans get set in concrete, it takes God a long time to melt them down.

The decision Lot made led to the downfall of the whole family. Let me caution you fathers to weigh prayerfully, cautiously and carefully every decision that you make. Measure that decision by the principles of God's Word.

When you make the right decision, the Devil will immediately rise up and fight you. When you make the wrong decision, the Devil won't bother you: you've made the decision he wanted you to make. But make the right decision, and immediately the forces of evil come in against you.

I caution you again to weigh every decision you make by the authority, the principles, the precepts, the teaching of God's Holy Word.

THE CAUSE OF BACKSLIDING

Consider why Lot and his family backslid. One simple word summarizes the reason—**greed**, just plain greed. Greed is the root of most problems and difficulties in families.

So the word that describes the backsliding of the family of Lot is greed. Greed motivated Lot to make the wrong choice in choosing "all the plain of Jordan." Why did he choose the plain of Jordan? Because it was well watered. I can imagine Lot said, "I can probably feed a thousand head of cattle and five hundred head of sheep on this rich land, along with a few goats. It produces well. It is well watered. This land is the best in the valley." Lot wanted the best for himself.

Sometimes what we think is best is not really what God wants for us. Lot's selfish attitude led him to make the wrong choice. From the standpoint of the world, it was an excellent choice. For an unbeliever, it could have become a tremendously profitable choice. But for believers, such as Lot, it was a *fatal* choice.

Basically, Lot was a good man, but he was motivated by selfish desires and worldly ambitions. Let me give you a danger signal: When you begin to be motivated by worldly ambitions and worldly desires, be careful!

"Love not the world, neither the things that are in the world. . . .

For all that is in the world, the lust of the flesh, and the lust of the eyes, and the pride of life, is not of the Father, but is of the world. And the world passeth away, and the lust thereof: but he that doeth the will of God abideth for ever."—I John 2:15–17.

The more like the world we are, the less like Jesus Christ we become. The closer we are to the world, the further we are from God. The more we become involved in worldly pursuits, the less involved we are in Christian service. We get bogged down, enamored and involved with worldly pursuits. When we get involved in them to the point that we lessen our involvement in the service of Christ, it becomes a detriment to our spiritual growth.

Lot's worldly ambition and covetous spirit led him and his family to a life totally devoid of spiritual influences. Lot made a decision. We can summarize the cause of backsliding with these three statements:

Selfish *aims*.

Selfish *ambitions*.

Selfish *aspirations*.

All of these stem from a greedy, selfish heart. Selfishness is so unlike Christianity. Selfishness is so unlike Christ, so unlike biblical principles. Not one word in the Scripture leads to selfishness; it all leads to a free spirit giving to God, to family, to the community, to everything. Jesus gave everything. What better example could we have? Don't let greed cause you to get away from God.

> Don't let greed cause you to get away from God.

THE COURSE OF BACKSLIDING

One word describes the course that Lot and his family

took in their backsliding—*gradual*. Backsliding never begins with a loud bang; it is always quiet, silent, subtle. In forty years of ministry, I have never had anyone say to me, "Preacher, I have just this morning decided to quit church, quit tithing, quit praying, quit on God." It never happens that way. It is a gradual process. No Christian plunges headlong into a backslidden condition. Backsliding is not a blowout; it is a slow leak.

> **Backsliding is not a blowout; it is a slow leak.**

Going downhill is always a gradual descent. You get in your car and drive to where there is a steep hill. You are on top of that hill. Nobody automatically goes to the bottom of that hill. You make a gradual descent until you reach the bottom. That is exactly what happens in spiritual things. You don't go immediately from the top of a spiritual experience to the bottom of a backslidden condition. It is a gradual course.

Let's construct a little scenario. Here is a family that is very active in church. But then some things come along, and the family decides, "Well now, Wednesday night is not really that important, so we will just stop attending on Wednesday night."

When they start missing the Wednesday night service, it is much easier to miss the Sunday night service. When they stop coming on Wednesday night and Sunday night, before long they will find themselves missing the Sunday morning service.

After awhile they will start neglecting prayer. "We don't have time to pray this morning; we will catch up tonight." Then after the late news and the late show, it is too late to pray. So their prayer life diminishes.

Before long they leave off their Bible reading. "We will catch up next week, for sure." But you know what happens next week.

Charles Haddon Spurgeon said, "Backsliding begins with dusty Bibles and ends with filthy garments."

Lay your Bible up on the shelf for just a little while, and you will get dirty. This is not an imaginary scenario; this is the truth. Families start missing church on Wednesday night, then start missing church on Sunday night, then on Sunday morning. Their prayer life is neglected; they postpone or quit reading the Bible altogether; then they stop witnessing; then they stop tithing; then—zap! It's all over. Oh, they may drop in to go to church once in awhile, when it is convenient. It is a gradual, downhill progression.

Such was the experience of Lot. His backsliding was gradual.

Lot **looked** toward Sodom—verse 10. His thinking probably was: *That land will make good crops. I can raise a lot of cattle on it.* Lot just looked toward Sodom.

Then he **leaned** toward Sodom—verse 12. He pitched his tent. He didn't move in all of a sudden. First he looked, then he pitched his tent in that city. Sodom didn't move toward him; he moved toward Sodom. Sodom didn't rise up and say, "I'm going to meet Lot halfway." Lot started looking, then he leaned in that direction, then he moved into Sodom.

It happened gradually because he took a first look. Some of you who are looking toward Sodom, looking toward sin, had better put your eyes back on Jesus.

He looked, he leaned. Then Lot **lived** in Sodom. Verse 12 says: " . . . Lot dwelled in the cities of the plain."

He looked, he leaned, he lived, then he **legislated** in Sodom. Chapter 19, verse 1, says: "And there came two angels to Sodom at even; and Lot sat in the gate of Sodom." Now he is not only looking, leaning and living; he is legislating. He has become one of the city fathers. In fact, farther on in chapter 19 they will say, "This one fellow came in to sojourn" [to stay only awhile]. No Christian intends to stay in the world forever. No one intends to get out there among the Devil's crowd and sell out and live with that crowd forever. He thinks, *One day I will get back in church. One day I will get right with God.* The Bible says Lot "sat in the gate." That means he was a judge or a city councilman or in some position of authority.

It all started with a look.

He looked, he leaned, he lived, he legislated in a wicked city; but listen to the tragedy of this: he **learned** the ways of Sodom. Sodomy is one of the greatest of sins. Read Romans, chapter 1, and see what God says about it. Read in the Old Testament, in the laws of God to Israel, what God said about sodomy. And remember what it says in Genesis 13:13: "But the men of Sodom were wicked and sinners before the LORD exceedingly."

In chapter 19, verses 1–11, we read:

"And there came two angels to Sodom at even; and Lot sat in the gate of Sodom: and Lot seeing them rose up to meet them; and he bowed himself with his face toward the ground;

"And he said, Behold now, my lords, turn in, I pray you, into your servant's house, and tarry all night, and wash your feet, and ye shall rise up early, and go on your ways."

It seems to me he is suggesting, "I will let you stay all night, but I will get you up early. I don't want angels around the house, because I have some things in the refrigerator that ought not be there. You may stay, but only a short while."

"And they said, Nay; but we will abide in the street all night [angels preferred spending the night in the street over spending it in the house of a backslidden believer].

"And he pressed upon them greatly [persuaded them]; *and they turned in unto him, and entered into his house; and he made them a feast, and did bake unleavened bread, and they did eat.*

"But before they lay down [went to bed], *the men of the city,* [homosexuals, sodomites, perverts], *even the men of Sodom, compassed the house round, both old and young, all the people from every quarter;*

"And they called unto Lot, and said unto him, Where are the men which came in to thee this night? bring them out unto us, that we may know them [that we may have a homosexual relationship with them; that we may commit sodomy with them].

"And Lot went out at the door unto them, and shut the door after him,

"And said, I pray you, brethren, do not so wickedly.

"Behold now, I have two daughters which have not known man; let me, I pray you, bring them out unto you, and do ye to them as is good in your eyes [do whatever you want to my two virgin daughters]; *only unto these men do nothing."*

When a man, a father, reaches that state, he has hit bottom. Spiritually he would have to reach up to touch the bottom. 'Take my two daughters, who are virgins, and do whatever you want with them; only don't do anything to these men.'

Lot was afraid that the wrath of God was going to fall on his house.

"And they said, Stand back. And they said again, This one

fellow came in to sojourn, and he will needs be a judge [he came to stay a little while; now he is one of the judges, one of the city councilmen]*: now will we deal worse with thee, than with them. And they pressed sore upon the man, even Lot, and came near to break the door.*

"*But the men put forth their hand, and pulled Lot into the house to them, and shut to the door.*

"*And they smote the men that were at the door of the house with blindness, both small and great: so that they wearied themselves to find the door.*"

Lot looked toward Sodom, he leaned toward Sodom, he lived in Sodom, he legislated in Sodom; now he has learned the ways of Sodom. The angels were reluctant to spend the night in the home of a backslidden believer.

Charles Haddon Spurgeon said, "When a house is ruled according to God's Word, if angels were asked to stay with us, they would not find themselves out of their element."

If angels showed up at our door, could we just open the door and say to them, "Come in; you will feel right at home in my house"?

By now, Lot was settled in. He was living among the sodomites in a comfortable lifestyle. Here is the danger. It is like a frog. Put him in a pail of water. When it gets a little warm, he doesn't feel the need of jumping out. Then it gets a little warmer. He still doesn't try to escape. It gets a little warmer, and a little warmer; then the water begins to boil, then it is . . . a stewed frog.

You get settled back into a little worldly living for a little while, and it doesn't seem so bad. Start missing church, and after awhile it doesn't bother you to miss church. Stop reading your Bible, and you lose the pangs of conscience about it. The same is true with tithing. The first Sunday when the offering plate is passed it drives you crazy. The next Sunday it is not quite so bad. After all, God didn't slice off a cloud and hit you in the head with it. So you think, *I will try not tithing again this week and see what happens.* First thing you know, you have settled down in a backslidden condition, away from God and out of fellowship with Him.

I warn you: be careful how you become comfortable in the world. In this world of unbelievers with their lifestyles, no Christian can really be comfortable. Romans 12:1,2 says to us:

"I beseech you therefore, brethren, by the mercies of God, that ye present your bodies a living sacrifice, holy, acceptable unto God, which is your reasonable service. And be not conformed to this world: but be ye transformed by the renewing of your mind, that ye may prove what is that good, and acceptable, and perfect, will of God."

May God help us not to become comfortable nor to feel at home in this world.

THE CONSEQUENCES OF BACKSLIDING

One word describes the consequences of backsliding—grave.

The consequence of backsliding is the grave.

Lot lost the companionship of his righteous uncle, Abraham. Chapter 13 says Abraham went one direction and Lot the other. Look at verse 11: "Then Lot chose him all the plain of Jordan." Why? It was well watered. Here we see greed, selfishness. Now look at Abraham in verses 14–18:

> "And the LORD said unto Abram, after that Lot was separated from him, Lift up now thine eyes, and look from the place where thou art northward, and southward, and eastward, and westward:
>
> "For all the land which thou seest, to thee will I give it, and to thy seed for ever.
>
> "And I will make thy seed as the dust of the earth: so that if a man can number the dust of the earth, then shall thy seed also be numbered.
>
> "Arise, walk through the land in the length of it and in the breadth of it; for I will give it unto thee.
>
> "Then Abram removed his tent, and came and dwelt in the plain of Mamre, which is in Hebron, and built there an altar unto the LORD."

Note the contrast. Lot chose the well-watered plains of the Jordan. What did he get in return? Zero. Abraham stood still before God. He had said to Lot, "You go the way you want. You make a choice; I will take what's left over." Lot made his choice, and God said, 'Abraham, because you have done the right thing, look northward, look southward, look eastward, look westward. I will give you and to your seed after you all that territory forever. I am going to bless you, and thousands will be born of your loins.'

It pays to serve Jesus; it pays every day;
It pays every step of the way.

Lot lost the companionship of his righteous uncle when he chose the cities of the plain—chose it for present pleasure and profit. Abraham chose a city that had foundations, whose builder and maker is God—chose it for future possession. Who got the better end of the deal?

This world is not my home; I'm just a passing through;
My treasures are laid up somewhere beyond the blue.
The angels beckon me from Heaven's open door,
And I can't feel at home in this world anymore.

Lot lost fellowship with God. Chapter 13, verse 13, says that the men of Sodom were wicked and sinners before God exceedingly. There was no altar in Sodom, no prayer meeting in Sodom, no worship service in Sodom, no holiness in Sodom. Lot did not win one single convert in Sodom. He lost fellowship with God.

Lot lost his testimony. Look again at chapter 19, verses 11–14:

"And they smote the men that were at the door of the house with blindness . . . .

"And the men said unto Lot, Hast thou here any besides? son in law, and thy sons, and thy daughters, and whatsoever thou hast in the city, bring them out of this place:

"For we will destroy this place, because the cry of them is waxen great before the face of the LORD; and the LORD hath sent us to destroy it.

"And Lot went out, and spake unto his sons in law, which married his daughters, and said, Up, get you out of this place: for the LORD will destroy this city. But he seemed as one that mocked unto his sons in law."

His sons-in-law said, "Old fool, don't tell us about God when you have never mentioned His name. We have never heard you mention righteousness. Nor have we ever seen you do anything right. Don't talk to us about divine intervention. We won't believe you!" They slammed the door in his face.

Lot had lost his testimony. One of the saddest things in all the world is for a Christian to lose his testimony. In gaining influence with the citizens of Sodom, he had lost influence with his own family.

J. Edgar Hoover said, "Children reared in homes where righteousness is taught and lived rarely become delinquents."

Lot lost his possessions. Look again at chapter 19, verses 24, 25:

> *"Then the Lord rained upon Sodom and upon Gomorrah brimstone and fire from the Lord out of heaven;*
> *"And he overthrew those cities, and all the plain, and all the inhabitants of the cities, and that which grew upon the ground."*

God burned up those well-watered plains that Lot looked upon, hoping to gain by them. He lost all of his possessions.

Lot lost his family. He lost his daughters. He lost his wife. Look at chapter 19, verse 26: "But his wife looked back from behind him, and she became a pillar of salt."

Don't look back! Don't look back to the sins, the mistakes, the heartaches, the problems. Don't look back toward the world. Look toward Jesus, the author and finisher of our faith.

If it could have been possible for Lot's wife to have come out of that pillar of salt, I believe Lot would have put his arms around her and said, "Honey, I forgive you for looking back." That is just like God, who is in the forgiving business.

What shall I say about this next loss?

Lot lost his self-respect. Verses 33 through 36 tell us that Lot, in a drunken stupor, committed incest with both daughters. Incest is happening more every day. The Bible says that Lot's righteous soul was vexed in Sodom. He couldn't be comfortable in Sodom. Neither can you nor I be comfortable in sin. Our souls will be vexed just like his was. Yet in spite of all he had, Lot lost his self-respect and committed incest with his own daughters in a drunken stupor.

God have mercy! It is unbelievable what men will do when they stoop to that place. I remind you that Lot didn't commit that wicked sin all of a sudden. He **looked**, he **leaned**, he **lived**, he **legislated**, he **learned** the ways of Sodom.

Here are seven danger signs to watch for in the disintegration of your family and home:

1. A **desire** to be like the world.

2. A **disaffection** for spiritual things. Anytime you start loving the things of the world more than you love the things of Christ, your affections have gone to the world, and you are disaffected from spiritual things.

3. A **disproportionate appropriation** of your family budget. If you are spending more money for pleasure and entertainment than you are for God, that is a disproportionate appropriation of your family's money, and God is going to judge you for it. Budget your money carefully and prayerfully. Make your investments in the cause of Christ first, and all these other things will be added.

4. A **disarmament** against the wiles of the Devil. Paul said, 'Having done all, to stand . . . against the wiles of the Devil.' As soon as we lay down our arms, the moment we disarm ourselves, the Devil comes right in and takes over.

5. A **diminishing involvement** in the program of the church. A lessening of your duties and responsibilities is a danger signal.

6. A **decline** in the regularity of family devotions. Every day, every family ought to have family devotions. A diminishing, a declining in the regularity of family devotions is a danger signal. It has been said that a family *altar* would *alter* many families.

7. A **disregard** for biblical principles. Don't ever say, "Well, the Bible is outdated, old-fashioned. It was meant for Moses, Abraham, Lot, Isaac, Daniel, Isaiah, Paul, James or John." Listen, it is meant for us, too. God's Word has not changed. He hasn't written another book.

Which will it be for your family? Sodom, with Lot; or Salem, with Abraham? Sodom had a purse, but it also had a curse. Oh, we know that before God destroyed the cities of Sodom and Gomorrah, God spared Lot from the awful destruction.

It was not until God had removed Lot from Sodom that He rained fire and overthrew the cities of Sodom and Gomorrah. Oh, that is the mercy of God!

God, in His mercy, is giving all of us an opportunity to get out of the world, to get out of Sodom, before judgment comes.

THE MARRIAGE MADE IN HEAVEN

–ISAAC–
Genesis 24:50–67

"Then Laban and Bethuel answered and said, The thing proceedeth from the Lord: we cannot speak unto thee bad or good.

"Behold, Rebekah is before thee, take her, and go, and let her be thy master's son's wife, as the Lord hath spoken.

"And it came to pass, that, when Abraham's servant heard their words, he worshipped the Lord, bowing himself to the earth.

"And the servant brought forth jewels of silver, and jewels of gold, and raiment, and gave them to Rebekah: he gave also to her brother and to her mother precious things.

"And they did eat and drink, he and the men that were with him, and tarried all night; and they rose up in the morning, and he said, Send me away unto my master.

"And her brother and her mother said, Let the damsel abide with us a few days, at the least ten; after that she shall go.

"And he said unto them, Hinder me not, seeing the Lord hath prospered my way; send me away that I may go to my master.

"And they said, We will call the damsel, and inquire at her mouth.

"And they called Rebekah, and said unto her, Wilt thou go with this man? And she said, I will go.

"And they sent away Rebekah their sister, and her nurse, and Abraham's servant, and his men.

"And they blessed Rebekah, and said unto her, Thou art our sister, be thou the mother of thousands of millions, and let thy seed possess the gate of those which hate them.

"And Rebekah arose, and her damsels, and they rode upon the

camels, and followed the man: and the servant took Rebekah, and went his way.

"And Isaac came from the way of the well Lahai-roi; for he dwelt in the south country.

"And Isaac went out to meditate in the field at the eventide: and he lifted up his eyes, and saw, and, behold, the camels were coming.

"And Rebekah lifted up her eyes, and when she saw Isaac, she lighted off the camel.

"For she had said unto the servant, What man is this that walketh in the field to meet us? And the servant had said, It is my master: therefore she took a vail, and covered herself.

"And the servant told Isaac all things that he had done.

"And Isaac brought her into his mother Sarah's tent, and took Rebekah, and she became his wife; and he loved her: and Isaac was comforted after his mother's death."

It was a happy day when Isaac first laid eyes on the girl of his dreams. It was love at first sight. She saw him, he saw her, and because God had already planned this, they were immediately in love.

Love is a wonderful thing. For a symphony of love, read I Corinthians 13. There God has His definition of *love*.

Love has no dimensions, no boundaries. It is deeper than the ocean, higher than the sky; loftier than the breeze of a spring morning. Love transcends reason. You don't explain love; you experience love. Love supersedes Herculean strength. Love comprehends the incomprehensible, moves the immovable, solves the unsolvable, answers the unanswerable, mends the unmendable. The love of a man for a woman and that of a woman for a man defies all logic as it runs the gamut from "A" to "Z." It is **a**mazing, **b**eautiful, **c**onquering, **d**esirable, **e**xcellent, **f**orever. Love is **g**ratifying, **h**eavenly, **i**ndescribable, **j**oyful, kind, long-suffering, magnificent, necessary. Love is opulent, precious, quantitative, royal; it is splendorous, terrific, universal, vivacious, wonderful; it is "x-acting," youthful, zestful!

What a delightful story of love accompanies the wedding! The occasion was a wedding purposefully planned and perfectly executed. This wedding was created and designed by God Himself—a wedding made in Heaven.

The questions came, "Shall she go? Should we send her away? What shall we do about this?" The answers are in verse 50: "Then Laban and Bethuel answered and said, The thing proceedeth from the LORD: we cannot speak unto thee bad or good." In other words, "We can't speak; we can't change what God has ordained."

> We can't change what God has ordained.

God had planned this marriage, putting it in the heart of Abraham to get a bride for his son Isaac. Not much is said about courtship in this case. The arrangements for marriages in those days were made by the parents. It wouldn't be a bad idea for parents today to say to their child early in a relationship, "Is this God's plan for your life? Or is this just some physical attraction, some fascination that you have about the opposite sex? Marriage is more than that."

Man has no right to rearrange or disannul what God arranges. The Lord hath spoken. Look at verse 51. They said, "Behold, Rebekah is before thee, take her, and go, and let her be thy master's son's wife, as the LORD hath spoken." So be it—willed of God, arranged by God, promoted by God, produced by God, and provided by the Lord Himself. Even marriages that are made in Heaven have to be lived out on earth. Because marriage is expressing itself in our lives among earthly environs, we must view it from a human standpoint.

I want to consider three things about marriage:

THE INSTITUTION OF MARRIAGE

Marriage is more than the execution of a civil contract. Anyone can go to a justice of the peace, lay down some money, get a license, and say, "Marry us." Marriage is more than that. The marriage ceremony is a service of worshipful celebration, the coming together of two devoted hearts that beat to the same rhythm. Marriage celebrates the union of two compatible personalities.

Let me give you an illustration. Hold a lump of dark blue clay in one hand and a lump of light blue clay in the other. Rub them together until they become one lump of clay. What do you see? Dark blue clay and light blue clay. Both colors are still visible and distinct, though they form one lump of clay.

When the married couple come together, it does not eradicate **her** personality, nor does it eradicate **his** personality. They are blended together into one. This is the oneness, the unity, the togetherness of marriage.

Marriage celebrates God's method of joining a man and a woman in the holy state of matrimony. No manner of living together is acceptable except God's divinely ordained method. You can't just say, "I am going to move in, and we will live together, and we will do what we want to do as husband and wife." Not in God's sight! When God brings you together, you go His way, the Bible way, the honorable way to join your lives together. That is what God says. It is of the Lord. It should be made in Heaven.

God ordained marriage before He formed any other

institution—before the church, governments, schools, businesses or anything else. God declared in Hebrews 13:4 that 'marriage is honorable and the bed of marriage undefiled.'

God instituted marriage for a threefold purpose:

1. To **propagate** the human race.
2. To **establish** a divine social order.
3. To **transmit holiness** from one generation to another.

Therefore, we must conclude that marriage lies at the basis of all human legislation, and upon it rests the peace and well-being of our nation. Destroy marriage, and you destroy the nation. Destroy the institution of marriage, and you destroy the world. If our nation is to survive, the institution of marriage must survive as ordained by God.

Jesus sanctioned the institution of marriage at the wedding of Cana of Galilee where He turned the water to wine. God blends lives together in a unity of body, soul and spirit. God performed the first wedding Himself in the Garden of Eden when He brought Adam and Eve together and united them in the first marriage ceremony. Because man and woman are bound together in body, soul and spirit, Adam said, "This is now bone of my bones, and flesh of my flesh."

God seals the marriage relationship with divine authority. He says in Genesis 2:24, "Therefore shall a man leave his father and his mother, and shall cleave unto his wife." *Cleave* means "to hang onto, be a part of, stay with."

Marriage celebrates the **commitment** of a man and woman, a commitment made willingly and voluntarily. The commitment is spelled out in the vows that are exchanged: "For better, for worse, for richer, for poorer, in sickness and in health, till death do us part." There is a "lock" in wedlock, according to God's holy ordinance.

The commitment is declared by the exchanging of the wedding rings. "With this ring I thee wed, and with all my worldly goods I thee endow in the name of the Father, the Son, and of the Holy Spirit." The wedding ring becomes a token, an outward symbol of the unity, the oneness, the togetherness, the bone of my bone, the flesh of my flesh, the heart of my heart, the life of my life, the spirit of my spirit. The commitment is publicized in the solemnity of the pronouncement: "I now pronounce you husband and wife, in the name of the Father, and of the Son, and of the Holy Spirit."

One new life exists in two individuals. It is blessed to see the unity candle used in a marriage ceremony. It symbolizes that two people have come into the sanctuary as two individuals, with different backgrounds and out of different families. So many things are different about them, yet so many things are alike that when they take their candles and light the unity candle they are saying, "We have become one in Jesus Christ." That is the institution of marriage.

THE INVOLVEMENTS OF MARRIAGE

Marriage involves looking for the best in your partner. You can look for what is bad, or you can look for what is good in your partner. Let me use an illustration of the buzzard and the bee. Their eating habits are far different.

The buzzard flies over the rubbish heap out in the field until he spots some decaying body; then he swoops down, picks it up, eats it, digests it and savors every bite.

You and I wouldn't dare go near that stinking, putrefying, rotten body; but the buzzard enjoys every morsel.

On the other hand, the bee flits throughout the garden, lands on a flower, pulls the sweet nectar from it, savoring every moment.

Which are you—buzzard or bee? Don't be a buzzard. Husband, look for something good in her. Wife, look for something good in him. Both of you will find what you are looking for.

God didn't say to the husband, "Love your wife until you discover something bad in her." He didn't say to the wife, "Be in subjection to your husband until you find something bad in him." If you look for something bad, you will find it. If you look for something good, you will find it. Whether you are celebrating your first anniversary or your fiftieth, you can either find some positive and pleasing component in your mate upon which to build some fond memories, or you can dig up some rotten garbage to satisfy your morbid appetite.

I repeat: don't be a buzzard. Look for some good traits, good characteristics, good attributes. Pluck the sweet nectar from the flower of your life.

Marriage involves submission and sacrifice. God says in Ephesians 5:22 and 23:

"Wives, submit yourselves unto your own husbands, as unto the Lord. For the husband is the head of the wife, even as Christ is the head of the church: and he is the saviour of the body."

Then in verse 25 He says to the husbands,

"Husbands, love your wives, even as Christ also loved the church, and gave himself for it."

He goes on to say that a man doesn't destroy his own

body, so why would he destroy his wife's? He nourishes and cherishes it even as Christ does the church.

What does submission mean? It does **not** mean slavery. It does **not** mean that a wife is a non-person. It does

> Submission is volunteered, not demanded.

not mean that she is without will, expression, or personality of her own. It does **not** mean that a wife is to be denied her gifts or talents. Just because God took the woman out of the side of the man doesn't mean she is only a "side issue." God did not take the woman out of his head, so he could lord it over her or be her "master"; nor out of his feet, so he could put her down and trample upon her; but He took woman out of his side, that he might love her.

A man is not complete without a woman, and a woman is not complete without a man. God took a part of man to make a woman. When God did that, man was never complete until He made a woman to fill what He had taken out of the man.

So the woman is made for the man, and the man for the woman, and neither is complete without the other. It takes that extra rib to make you husbands whole. Wives, it took that rib to make you originally. "Bone of my bone," Adam said, "and flesh of my flesh." That does not mean the wife should be denied her expression. Often her wisdom and insight are far keener than that of her husband.

What does submission mean? It means arranging one's self under the scriptural authority of another. Submission is volunteered, not demanded. Husbands, if you have to say every third day, "I am the king of this castle," you are not king of this castle. You may be occupying the place, but you are really not king. Submission is putting yourself under the scriptural authority of another.

Husbands, you will make submission much easier as you express the quality of love described in Ephesians 5:22, 23. These verses suggest five ways that Christ loved the church, and Paul tells husbands to love their wives in these five ways:

1. Realistically;
2. Sacrificially;
3. Purposefully;
4. Willfully;
5. Absolutely.

The proper scriptural relationship is dual. Submission means that the wife is to trust, respect and honor her husband as he displays the quality of sacrificial love that Christ has for the church, for **leadership** minus love equals **tyranny**. The wife's submission is to Jesus Christ through the life of her husband.

Paul draws the parallel between the church and the wife, and the husband and Christ. As Christ is head over the church and the church is in submission to Christ, so the husband is the head of the wife, and the wife is in submission to him. That is the way God set it up: God, Jesus Christ the Son, and the church.

Now, don't miss this. *The role of the head of the home is successfully implemented* **only** *when the husband assumes the position of a servant who is motivated by love, as exemplified in the attitude of Jesus Christ toward the church for which He gave Himself in death.* Are you fulfilling that role?

Marriage involves dedication and devotion. What appears to be a **dream** can be turned into a **nightmare** unless there are sincere dedication and a meaningful devotion on the part of both partners. The husband's dedication and devotion to his wife are essential. Husband, shield your wife from the rough and raging storms of life. Cling to her with unwavering fidelity. Cherish her emotionally and physically with unfailing affection. Guard her happiness with unceasing vigilance. Consider your wife the weaker vessel as described in I Peter 3:7.

Wife, what about your dedication, your devotion to your husband? Do you honor him by satisfying his emotional and physical needs? Do you understand that a husband's needs are not the same as yours? God didn't make you alike. Sustain your husband by supporting his aims and aspirations. Nothing is more debilitating and humiliating than for a woman to degrade her husband—the way he thinks, the way he talks, the way he walks, the way he lives, the way he works, or where he works. Don't destroy whatever your husband has for you. Don't be guilty of degrading him. Handle your husband with tender, loving care. A reading of Proverbs 31:10–31 would be helpful.

> It takes three to make a satisfying marriage: God, husband and wife.

It takes **three** to make a satisfying marriage: God, husband and wife. You think you know some unsaved people who do well. I am not talking about unsaved people, but about saved people—you and me. It takes three persons: God, a husband and a wife. It is a **triangular** arrangement, a three-dimensional situation; and all three parties must be consulted in all decisions, in all assessments, in all plans, in all actions. Ecclesiastes 4:12 reminds us, "A threefold cord is not quickly broken." God, husband, wife—a three-dimensional situation, and all three are to be consulted in every action.

Husband, shame on you if you go around boasting, "I

don't ask my wife anything." You are not a husband; you are a male occupying the place of a husband. Why don't you ask your wife's advice? She probably has more good wisdom, more good sense than you. Don't think you have to make every decision, every assessment, every judgment by yourself. I never buy a pair of socks, shirt or suit without my wife's helping me pick it out. We make decisions and assessments together.

Talk about where you are going to live on your knees before God. Where you can make the most money is not always the best place to live. Talk together with God about what kind of house you are going to buy, what kind of car you want to drive, the places you prefer to visit, the people with whom you will associate.

Marriage is beautiful, satisfying and enduring only if God is in it. "Except the LORD build the house, they labour in vain that build it."

We can have all the building materials; we may have attended all the seminars, but for the answer, look in the Bible. Our problem is that we are too lazy to get it down and find the answer. God's Word has all the answers. He said, "If any of you lack wisdom, let him ask of God." Ask God how to bring up your children in the right way. Certainly you need help, especially in these days when there are so many things pulling at you. Get the answers from God's Word instead of running everywhere trying to find out who is going to say what next.

God said that it is not good for a human being to be alone. After everything He made, He said, 'It is good.' Then He said, "It is **not** good that the man should be alone." So what did He do? He made "an help meet for him." Don't misquote the Scripture; it is a help **meet**, not a help **mate**. He made somebody conditioned to help him, meet to help him, trained, characterized, made in order to help him, one who can meet his needs.

It is a tragedy that many men and women are alone even in marriage.

Here is a tragedy: many a man and woman are alone even in marriage, and that results in undue suffering. If we would go God's way, we could spare ourselves a lot of suffering and heartache.

God created man and woman for intimacy in marriage. There are more ways of being intimate than the sex act. A man who thinks that sex is the only way he can be intimate with his wife is only a brute with an insatiable sexual appetite. What about a warm smile, a soft squeezing of the hand, a tender touch, an affectionate kiss on the cheek, an assuring hug, an "I love you. I need you. I want you. I would give my life for you"? Talk about getting intimate! That gets intimate. Intimacy is reflected in a strong personal relationship. Intimacy provides security, cultivates unity and promotes friendship. The key to intimacy with each other is an **intimate relationship** with Jesus Christ. That is when it is sanctified, when it is holy, when it is not just for physical gratification.

The Christian marriage can be defined as a total commitment of two people to the Person and Lordship of Jesus Christ and to each other. It is a commitment in which there is a pledge of mutual fidelity. It is a commitment to a partnership of mutual subordination. It is a commitment to a mutual refinement of each other in the light of God's Word.

You and I ought to strive to bring out the best in our partners. Don't be a buzzard digging for the garbage, digging for the unpleasant. Pluck the sweet nectar from the flower of your life.

God says:

"Therefore shall a man leave his father and his mother, and shall cleave unto his wife: and they shall be one flesh."—Gen. 2:24.

Jesus says:

"It hath been said, Whosoever shall put away his wife, let him give her a writing of divorcement: But I say unto you, That whosoever shall put away his wife, saving for the cause of fornication, causeth her to commit adultery: and whosoever shall marry her that is divorced committeth adultery."—Matt. 5:31,32.

Paul says:

"For this cause shall a man leave his father and mother, and shall be joined unto his wife, and they two shall be one flesh. This is a great mystery: but I speak concerning Christ and the church. Nevertheless let every one of you in particular so love his wife even as himself; and the wife see that she reverence her husband."—Eph. 5:31–33.

The marriage union is not one ego giving in to another ego. It is both egos surrendering to the will of God and uniting in Jesus Christ. It is Jesus Christ who makes the difference.

THE INGREDIENTS IN MARRIAGE

"We have a perfect marriage," you say. Not so! There is no perfect marriage, but we ought to strive to make ours perfect. Marriage is not a ready-made product; it is a day-to-day creation.

I ask every young couple who comes to my office for premarital counseling, "Are you in love?" Of course the answer is yes. I don't know why I ask such a stupid question when it shows all over them. Then I look the man and the woman right straight in the eye, and I say, " Five years from now, you ought be more in love than you are right now. Twenty-five years from now you ought to be more in love than you are right now. Fifty years from now, you ought to be more in love than you are right now."

It doesn't come automatically. When dating, you are on your best behavior: clean breath, clean fingernails, no smelly socks, pulling out the chair for her to sit down, opening the door for her to get in the car, taking off your coat and putting it over a mud puddle so she can step on it to go across. After you are married about three months, you don't open the car door for her. You don't go around and pull out the chair for her.

You are riding down the highway. She is over against the door—as far away from you as she can possibly get. You just drive on, looking solemn.

She says, "O John, it just isn't like it used to be. When we first got married, we sat so close together."

You answer, "Who has moved? I am right where I have always been."

We laugh, but it is little things that really count. (After forty-four years of marriage, I am beginning to learn how to be more considerate. I wish I had started it forty-four years ago.) Most of us are falling short in our relationships. It is those little things from day to day that cause us to get caught in Satan's trap. But this doesn't have to end a relationship that is built on the Word of God and united in Jesus Christ.

The first ingredient of marriage is love. Love is more than physical attraction that leads to sexual satisfaction.

True love is an emotional and spiritual attachment that grows stronger and deeper with the passing of time.

> True love is an emotional and spiritual attachment that grows stronger and deeper with the passing of time.

- ❤ **Love** is the **glue** that unites two hearts together and keeps marriages from falling apart.
- ❤ **Love** is the **catalyst** that sparks an otherwise dull relationship.
- ❤ **Love** is the **oil** that lubricates the friction areas between two differing personalities.
- ❤ **Love** is the **cord** that binds two maverick spirits into a union of one spirit in Jesus Christ.

The second ingredient of marriage is friendship. Your wife or your husband should be your best friend. The best friend I have is my wife. Nobody would have put up with me like she has for forty-four years, for I am not the easiest person in the world to live with. I am saying that friendship is a part of marriage. A husband and wife should be best friends as well as great lovers.

Enduring friendship is the **hallmark** of a happy marriage. If she is not your friend, she is not going to be much else. If he is not your friend, forget it.

> Enduring friendship is the hallmark of a happy marriage.

Friendship between married partners has steered many a ship over troubled waters. Someone said, "The difference between smooth sailing and shipwreck in marriage lies in what you as a couple are doing about the rough weather." Friendship is the **bridge** that spans the gap of marital differences.

The third ingredient of marriage is respect.

- ❤ Respect for each other is the **key** that opens the door to a healthy relationship.
- ❤ Respect builds **trust** and **confidence**.
- ❤ Respect engenders **admiration**, fosters **credibility**, promotes **compatibility**.

The fourth ingredient of marriage is communication. Communication is the **conduit** through which ideas and feelings pass freely from one partner to another. Don't allow your holy wedlock to become an "unholy deadlock."

You say, "Well, I just can't talk." Yes, you can talk. You talk to others about the weather, sports, politics, government, and your job. You can talk if you want to talk. The reason you don't talk to your partner is that you don't want to talk. No marriage will survive without communication.

Communication is a **dialogue**, not a **monologue**. Communication provides an outlet for pent-up emotions which otherwise could erupt into verbal explosions. Don't wait until you are so mad that you could just beat him up, or beat her up, or kick him out the window, or kick her out the door, or whatever. Start talking about your problem while it is still small. Sometimes communication is silent—a smile, a nod, a lifted eyebrow.

Communication generates understanding. That which is "talked out" can usually be "worked out." Talk about it. Communication erases **doubts** and **fears**. Communication reduces **suspicion** and strengthens **confidence**.

> The most important ingredient of marriage is forgiveness.

The fifth ingredient of marriage is forgiveness. Among the ingredients of marriage, the most important is forgiveness.

To err is human; to forgive is divine.

- Forgiveness is a clear-cut and logical choice on the part of the offended party.

- Forgiveness should not be contingent upon one partner's promising never to make the same mistake again. Nobody can promise that. Wife, don't you say to your husband, "If you promise me you will never do it again, I will forgive you." He can't promise you that. If you put conditions on forgiveness, then it is not forgiveness at all. Husband, don't say to your wife, "If you won't ever do that again, I will forgive you." She can't promise you that. **Conditional** forgiveness is **partial** forgiveness.

- Forgiveness is not just a feeling; it is a clear-cut choice. It is saying, "I love you, and I believe in you."

- Forgiveness is exercising trust in your partner.

- Forgiveness is accepting the worst and hoping for the best.

Love, respect, friendship, communication, forgiveness—these are the ingredients of marriage.

NEVER AND ALWAYS

Let me conclude with some *"nevers"* and some *"always."*

1. Some *"nevers"* for every marriage:

    - Never be intolerant of your mate's diverse ideas.
    - Never criticize your mate in public.
    - Never store up anger or accusations that you can "drop like a bomb" at some convenient time for you.

- Never clog the lines of communication with your mate.
- Never belittle your mate's family members.
- Never take your mate for granted.
- Never refuse to listen to your mate.
- Never be insensitive to your mate's feelings or moods.
- Never magnify your mate's faults or weaknesses.
- Never rehearse your mate's past failures.
- Never ignore your mate's warning signs of a breakdown in your relationship. If either begins to put out some warning signs and raise some red flags, sit up and take notice.
- Never attempt to reshape your mate's personality or remold your mate's disposition. Many a man has wrecked his marriage because he has tried to remake his wife after his own image. After all, God made her a different personality. Woman, you can't make your husband after your image. Remember the dark clay and the light clay. They come together as one clay. You can still see the light, you can still see the dark, but they are together.

2. Some *"always"* for every marriage:
   - Always consider your mate's feelings.
   - Always regard your mate as your partner in marriage, not your subordinate in business.
   - Always give your mate the benefit of the doubt.

- Always follow through with the commitments that you make to your mate.
- Always handle your mate's emotions with sincere regard.
- Always practice forgiveness toward your mate and allow time for healing.
- Always build up confidence in your mate's ability to achieve.
- Always prefer your mate's desires above your own.
- Always exercise care and understanding in approaching your mate's mistakes and misgivings.
- Always maximize your mate's strong points and minimize the weak ones.
- Always refrain from outbursts of anger when dissatisfied with your mate's performance.
- Always discern your mate's mood before communicating a problem. Don't take a problem to your mate when she or he is not in the mood for it. It complicates the problem; it doesn't solve it. "Read" the mood and then bring the problem to the surface.

SUMMARY

When two people are joined in marriage in Jesus Christ, they are united forever.

- Forever one,
- Forever in love,
- Forever partners,

- Forever lovers,
- Forever friends,
- Forever companions,
- Forever together.

God's divine plan—one man, one woman, for a lifetime. Such a marriage is made in Heaven. With all of our shortcomings, our faults, our failures, whatever he or she has done, you must say, "I love you. I believe in you. We can work it out with God's help." The divorce courts will not be nearly so crowded when we get this right.

Will you pray daily, *"God, make me a better spouse"*? May God help us to salvage our homes.

THE FAMILY WHO CAME BACK TO GOD

—JACOB—
Genesis 35:1–15

"And God said unto Jacob, Arise, go up to Beth-el, and dwell there: and make there an altar unto God, that appeared unto thee when thou fleddest from the face of Esau thy brother.

"Then Jacob said unto his household, and to all that were with him, Put away the strange gods that are among you, and be clean, and change your garments:

"And let us arise, and go up to Beth-el; and I will make there an altar unto God, who answered me in the day of my distress, and was with me in the way which I went.

"And they gave unto Jacob all the strange gods which were in their hand, and all their earrings which were in their ears; and Jacob hid them under the oak which was by Shechem.

"And they journeyed: and the terror of God was upon the cities that were round about them, and they did not pursue after the sons of Jacob.

"So Jacob came to Luz, which is in the land of Canaan, that is, Beth-el, he and all the people that were with him.

"And he built there an altar, and called the place El-beth-el: because there God appeared unto him, when he fled from the face of his brother.

"But Deborah Rebekah's nurse died, and she was buried beneath Beth-el under an oak: and the name of it was called Allon-bachuth.

"And God appeared unto Jacob again, when he came out of Padan-aram, and blessed him.

"And God said unto him, Thy name is Jacob: thy name shall not

be called any more Jacob, but Israel shall be thy name: and he called his name Israel.

"And God said unto him, I am God Almighty: be fruitful and multiply; a nation and a company of nations shall be of thee, and kings shall come out of thy loins;

"And the land which I gave Abraham and Isaac, to thee I will give it, and to thy seed after thee will I give the land.

"And God went up from him in the place where he talked with him.

"And Jacob set up a pillar in the place where he talked with him, even a pillar of stone: and he poured a drink-offering thereon, and he poured oil thereon.

"And Jacob called the name of the place where God spake with him, Beth-el."

What a delightful experience to see families together in the house of God! The church is the house of God, not a social club. It is not a place to take care of all your social engagements. Church is not a place for children to run and play. It is not a place to exchange ideas one with another while the choir is singing and the preacher is preaching. Church is not a place to eat candy and chew gum.

"God said . . . ." God spoke to a man. God is speaking to us, not in an audible voice but from the pages of His Word. There will be no extra-biblical revelation, no angels at the foot of the bed, no special writing in the sky. He has already given us sixty-six books. He has already spoken. "God said . . . ."

Notice to whom God spoke: "God said unto Jacob." Jacob is the father of a family. Husbands, God works through you. He did not say to Mrs. Jacob, "I want you to build an altar." God instructed the head of that family, the head of that home to do that. Fathers, you and

I ought always to be sensitive to the voice of God because He is speaking to us.

"And God said unto Jacob, Arise, go up to Beth-el, [go back] and dwell there: and make there an altar unto God." This was serious business between God and Jacob. God said, 'Build an altar at Bethel and stay there.' Jacob said, 'I will.' He didn't put up any argument. When God speaks, don't try to rationalize and reason God out of what He is saying. Rather, say, "Yes, Lord, I will."

Why should we attend church on Sunday morning, Sunday night and Wednesday night? Because God said we should. Why should we go and knock on doors and witness and win souls? Because God said we should. Why should we bring our tithes and offerings? Because God said we should. Why should we have a family altar? Because God said we should. Don't argue with God. Don't try to get Him to fashion His robe of righteousness to fit you. Put yourself in a position where He can tailor your life so His robe of righteousness fits right on you.

When He spoke to Jacob, Jacob said, 'I will.'

Jacob, one of the most colorful characters in all the Bible, is the son of Isaac and the brother of Esau. Any kind of description of him almost defies imagination. He was a schemer! He was a supplanter! In fact, *Jacob* means "supplanter" or "one who takes the place of another." He took the place of Esau. He connived with his father-in-law.

God said to him, "Thy name is Jacob [supplanter]: thy name shall not be called any more Jacob, but Israel [a prince with God] shall be thy name." No longer is he Jacob, but a prince with God. Every born-again believer is a prince with God.

Jacob's family was among the most famous of all the

patriarchal families. In fact, his sons make up the twelve tribes of Israel. His family not only made **history**, but they also provided the materials for **prophecy**. For God said to Jacob, "A nation . . . and kings shall come out of thy loins." Jacob was an unusual man who had an unusual mission in life.

Jacob's family did some things that all families need to do. I call his family "The Family Who Came Back to God." God had said, 'Go back to Beth-el.' You don't go back to some place unless you have left that place. It is a good thing to get right with God. It is a good thing for families to get on their faces before God. It is a good thing for families to gather around the Bible at home and fellowship in God's Word. In order for a family to get right with God, three things are necessary.

1. **Certain things have to be given up.** You and I cannot take all that we have enjoyed before our salvation and bring it over into our arena of Christian living. Some things have to be given up, turned loose. But remember, it is not what we **leave** but what we **receive** that causes us to rejoice as we live for Christ.

2. **You have to be in a certain place.** I believe God has a place of blessing. He said to Elijah, "Go to this place; and when you are there, I will bless you." If we are three feet away from where we ought to be, God will not bless us. We have to be in the place where God wants us in order to have the capacity to receive what God wants to give us.

3. **Certain things have to be done.** Children do not grow up to know Jesus Christ as their personal Saviour automatically. We don't just say, "I think I'm going to have a wonderful Christian family." You have to work at it. You have to pray. You have to read the Scriptures. You

have to be in church. You have to serve God. You have to bring your family where you want them to be. That is why God told Jacob, the head of that family, 'This is the way it has to be.'

Let us observe some things that Jacob's family did on their way back to God and back to the house of worship.

JACOB DID AWAY WITH IDOLS

"And God said unto Jacob, Arise, go up to Beth-el, and dwell there: and make there an altar unto God, that appeared unto thee when thou fleddest from the face of Esau thy brother.

"Then Jacob said unto his household, and to all that were with him, Put away the strange gods that are among you."—Gen. 35:1, 2.

An idol is anything that takes God's place. Anything becomes an idol that takes your devotion, your affection, your love that should be given to God.

"And God spake all these words, saying,

"I am the LORD thy God, which have brought thee out of the land of Egypt, out of the house of bondage.

"Thou shalt have no other gods before me.

"Thou shalt not make unto thee any graven image, or any likeness of any thing that is in heaven above, or that is in the earth beneath, or that is in the water under the earth.

"Thou shalt not bow down thyself to them, nor serve them: for I the LORD thy God am a jealous God, visiting the iniquity of the fathers upon the children unto the third and fourth generation of them that hate me;

"And shewing mercy unto thousands of them that love me, and keep my commandments."—Exod. 20:1–6.

The sin of idol worship had affected every member of

Jacob's family. Everything you do as head of your home affects your family. It affects your children. If they see one standard in you, hear another at church, another somewhere else, they get confused. Every idol, every pagan god, everything that takes God's place, affects the whole family. Jacob charged the whole family to get rid of **all** the idols.

There are many idols that families are worshiping. Many Christian families are worshiping the idol of **pleasure**. Many Christians care more for pleasure than they do for God or God's house. Look at their attendance records. On Sundays many churches have few in attendance because their members are out on the golf course, fishing, or taking care of some business that could have been taken care of at another time. Money, possessions and popularity have become gods. God said, "Thou shalt have no other gods before me."

The first thing Jacob's family did was to get rid of **all** the idols. They quit using God's holy day to do their own thing and started using it to do God's holy things.

A reckoning day is coming. We can't treat God's house and God's day any way we want and expect to get by with it. We cannot even do good things to the exclusion of the best thing. The best thing is to get the family in the house of God. Our homes, our children, our cars, our boats, our pleasures, our money, our materials, our popularity and fame can easily become idols if we give our affection and devotion and love to them rather than to God.

Put away **all** idol gods.

JACOB CHANGED HIS LIFESTYLE

Jacob's family changed their lifestyle. Look at the second part of verse 2. The first part was to put away the strange gods; the second part was "be clean, and change your garments."

In summertime we want to get comfortable. We want to be cool. Did you know that the more clothes you take off, the hotter you get? Ask Uncle Sam if that is not true. He keeps clothes on soldiers so when the wind hits them the perspiration will cool the body. Don't tell me you take off your clothes to get comfortable! You take them off so you can show off your body.

Don't you go to church for any activity half-naked. Paul says in I Timothy 2:9, "In like manner also, that women adorn themselves in modest apparel." Nakedness of body is not modest apparel. No one ought to wear short shorts. Jacob said to his family, "Be clean, and change your garments." Don't go around in indecent attire. Be modest in all your apparel. Dress as you would dress in the presence of Jesus Christ, for after all, He is present all the time. When a family gets away from | **Christians should look, live and love like Christians.** | God and church, it has a tendency to degenerate to a pagan and worldly lifestyle. Anytime we leave Bethel, leave the house of God, leave righteousness, the tendency is to take on the lifestyle of the world.

Christians ought to look, live and love like Christians. Why were they called Christians to start with? Because they went around bragging on what they had done? No. They were first called Christians in Antioch because people said, "They must be Christ-ones." A Christian is a Christ-one. Paul said in II Corinthians 6:17,18:

89

"Wherefore come out from among them, and be ye separate, saith the Lord, and touch not the unclean thing; and I will receive you. And will be a Father unto you, and ye shall be my sons and daughters, saith the Lord Almighty."

Jacob had to call for separation—clean up and change your clothes. He wanted them to look right, walk right, live right, talk right.

Dr. J. Frank Norris said, "When I see something that walks like a duck, and waddles like a duck, and quacks like a duck, I call it a duck." If I see something that looks like the world, smells like the world, walks like the world, and talks like the world, I am inclined to call it a worldling.

There has to come a time when we draw a line in the sand and step to the right side of it. God doesn't want us to be spiritual nuts but fruit-bearing Christians. If we are going to change the world, we have to shine like **lights** and shake like **salt**. If you want to become acclimated to the world and absorbed into the world, just live as you want to live, dress as you want to dress, go anywhere you want to go, do anything you want to do. But if you are out to change the world, you have to be different from what you are going to change. If you and I are not changing the world, then the world is changing us.

JACOB REMEMBERED WHAT GOD HAD DONE

Have you ever sat down and made a list of all the things God has done for you? Do you not remember anything He has done for you lately? You are breathing, aren't you? You are living, aren't you?

Verse 3 says, "And let us arise, and go up to Beth-el; and I will make there an altar unto God, who answered me in the day of my distress, and was with me in the way which I went." Here we see God's deliverance and God's presence. God delivered Jacob when he was in distress; God was with him when he was headed away from his brother, Esau.

How soon we forget! Never forget all the things God has done for you. Psalm 103:1, 2 says,

"Bless the Lord, O my soul: and all that is within me, bless his holy name. Bless the Lord, O my soul, and forget not all his benefits."

David begins naming some of those benefits: forgiveness, redemption, food—the good things God had done for him. Jacob did not forget, nor did he let his family forget, what God had done for them.

Father, sit down once in awhile and say, "Kids, look what God has done for us," and start naming what He has done. Of course, you can't name all His blessings, but list a few. Look at Deuteronomy 8:11–17:

"Beware that thou forget not the LORD thy God, in not keeping his commandments, and his judgments, and his statutes, which I command thee this day:

"Lest when thou hast eaten and art full and hast built goodly houses, and dwelt therein;

"And when thy herds and thy flocks multiply, and thy silver and thy gold is multiplied, and all that thou hast is multiplied;

"Then thine heart be lifted up, and thou forget the LORD thy God, which brought thee forth out of the land of Egypt, from the house of bondage;

"Who led thee through that great and terrible wilderness, wherein were fiery serpents, and scorpions, and drought, where there was no water; who brought thee forth water out of the rock of flint;

"Who fed thee in the wilderness with manna, which thy fathers

91

knew not, that he might humble thee, and that he might prove thee, to do thee good at thy latter end;

"And thou say in thine heart, My power and the might of mine hand hath gotten me this wealth."

Do you have money? God gave you the power to get it. Do you have a job? God gave it to you. Do you have food on the table? God gave it to you. Do you have clothes on your back? God gave them to you. Isn't God good? Don't ever forget His goodness!

Now verses 18–20:

"But thou shalt remember the LORD thy God: for it is he that giveth thee power to get wealth, that he may establish his covenant which he sware unto thy fathers, as it is this day.

"And it shall be, if thou do at all forget the LORD thy God, and walk after other gods, and serve them, and worship them, I testify against you this day that ye shall surely perish.

"As the nations which the LORD destroyeth before your face, so shall ye perish; because ye would not be obedient unto the voice of the LORD your God."

Don't ever forget what God has done for you!

JACOB RETURNED TO GOD AND THE ALTAR

Look at Genesis 35:6: "So Jacob came to Luz, which is in the land of Canaan, that is, Beth-el, he and all the people that were with him." In verses 1, 3 and 6 it is Bethel; but in verse 7: "And called the place El-Beth-el: because there God appeared unto him." He built an altar at Bethel, the house of God. An altar speaks of worship, of sacrifice, of devotion.

Is there an altar in your life? in your home? We have

room for everything else in the house: television, VCR, telephone, radio, stereo, microwave and all the rest. None of these is bad; but where is the altar, a place where you can say, "This is my home altar, the place where I get down on my knees, the place where the family comes together for worship"?

It doesn't all happen in church. We are living in a brainwashed age. Television is brainwashing this generation. God's people are sitting around watching religious television and seeing all of that "hoopla," then

> **It is the God of the church who is important.**

going to church and criticizing. "What is wrong with the preacher? What has happened?" You would be better off just reading your Bible than listening to most of what we get on these so-called "religious channels." Most of it will brainwash us to the point that, if somebody isn't jumping over the benches at church and screaming, hollering and foaming at the mouth, we will say, "What has happened to our church?"

If we really want to know, we should look in the mirror. If we don't see the altar lined with souls getting saved, don't blame it all on the preacher. Look in the mirror. I am talking about having an altar. I am talking about getting serious about this business of serving God.

Verse 7 says he called the place *El-Bethel*, meaning "the God of the house of God." We have desecrated God in the name of religion. You hear it said, "Give Jesus a hand." He doesn't need a hand! We have desecrated the holy God by bringing Him down to where we are and talking about Him as though He were a buddy of ours.

When people tell me they know exactly what God wants them to do twenty-four hours a day, I know something is wrong. Many times we have to make a few mistakes or a wrong decision, then God shows us. But nobody has a prescription from God, a road map from God, a plan from God, that enables him to say, "I know this is the way; nothing else is right."

Even Ruth in the Old Testament didn't know where she was going when she started, but God directed her. She thought it was by sheer chance that she got into Boaz's field, but God was working. She didn't say to Naomi, "I know exactly where Boaz lives. I am going right to his field and start gleaning right where Boaz is because I am going to get into the family of the Lord Jesus, and I am going to be there when . . ." Ruth didn't know any of that. The only thing she knew was that she wanted a place to labor, and God put her in the right place.

All you have to know is that you want a place to serve God, and God will put you in the right place.

Bethel means "house of God"; *El-Bethel* means "the God of the house of God." It is God, the great *I Am That I Am*, the God of the church, who is important.

It is easy to get caught up in the traditions and trappings of the church and forget who God is—"having a form of godliness, but denying the power thereof." The focus must be on God, not just on the house of God. The focus must be on the God of Abraham, Isaac and Jacob. The focus must be on the God and Father of our Lord Jesus Christ. It must be on the God of holiness, purity and righteousness. It must be on the God who saves, sanctifies and secures. It must be on the God who gives us light, life, love, liberty and power. It must be on the God of the valley as well as the God of the mountain.

It is not hard to serve God when all the children are well, when we are drawing a good paycheck, when we have CDs in the bank, a closet full of clothes, a cupboard full of food. It is never hard to serve Him while on a mountaintop. But what about the valley—the valley of despair, the valley of discouragement, the valley of despondency, the valley of disillusionment, the valley of disappointment, the valley of depression?

The number one illness in America is depression. The problem is, most people don't know why they are depressed. In many cases, much of it is a spiritual problem. Don't be taken in by those fellows who tell you, "Just send me ten dollars, and God's going to send you a thousand." The same God who is good up on a mountaintop is good down in the valley. "Yea, though I walk through the valley of the shadow of death, I will fear no evil: for thou art with me."

God is good while you're on the sickbed, good when life is broken, when dreams are scattered, when hearts are shattered, and when lives are torn apart. Put your eyes on Jesus, who goes with us to the river, then meets us on the other side. Faith in God is not some flighty thing, something that you dreamed up or conjured up in your emotionalism. A solid faith in the true and living God will take you through the storms, through the problems, through the heartaches, through the broken valleys of life. Keep your eyes on Him.

All of our families should follow the example that Jacob followed in getting back to the foundations of faith.

A poet said,

> Turn back to where you left Him,
> And you will find Him there.

95

He is waiting by your bedside,
　　Where you used to kneel in prayer.
He is standing in the chapel,
　　By that long-abandoned pew.
You are older, wiser, broken;
　　You're tired of self, 'tis true.
So return to where you left Him:
　　He's waiting there for you.

Return to Bethel, to the God of the house of God, and to the altar of prayer. Put away the idols in your life. Change your lifestyle. Remember what God has done for you!

A FAMILY SHAKEUP

–JOSEPH–
Genesis 37:1–17

"And Jacob dwelt in the land wherein his father was a stranger, in the land of Canaan.

"These are the generations of Jacob. Joseph, being seventeen years old, was feeding the flock with his brethren; and the lad was with the sons of Bilhah, and with the sons of Zilpah, his father's wives: and Joseph brought unto his father their evil report.

"Now Israel [Jacob] loved Joseph more than all his children, because he was the son of his old age: and he made him a coat of many colours.

"And when his brethren saw that their father loved him more than all his brethren, they hated him, and could not speak peaceably unto him.

"And Joseph dreamed a dream, and he told it his brethren: and they hated him yet the more.

"And he said unto them, Hear, I pray you, this dream which I have dreamed:

"For, behold, we were binding sheaves in the field, and, lo, my sheaf arose, and also stood upright; and, behold, your sheaves stood round about, and made obeisance to my sheaf.

"And his brethren said to him, Shalt thou indeed reign over us? or shalt thou indeed have dominion over us? And they hated him yet the more for his dreams, and for his words.

"And he dreamed yet another dream, and told it his brethren, and said, Behold, I have dreamed a dream more; and, behold, the sun and the moon and the eleven stars made obeisance to me.

"And he told it to his father, and to his brethren: and his father rebuked him, and said unto him, What is this dream that thou hast dreamed? Shall I and thy mother and thy brethren indeed come to *bow down ourselves to thee to the earth?*

"*And his brethren envied him; but his father observed the saying.*

"*And his brethren went to feed their father's flock in Shechem.*

"*And Israel said unto Joseph, Do not thy brethren feed the flock in Shechem? come, and I will send thee unto them. And he said to him, Here am I.*

"*And he said to him, Go, I pray thee, see whether it be well with thy brethren, and well with the flocks; and bring me word again. So he sent him out of the vale of Hebron, and he came to Shechem.*

"*And a certain man found him, and, behold, he was wandering in the field: and the man asked him, saying, What seekest thou?*

"*And he said, I seek my brethren: tell me, I pray thee, where they feed their flocks.*

"*And the man said, They are departed hence; for I heard them say, Let us go to Dothan. And Joseph went after his brethren, and found them in Dothan.*"

This is a remarkable and unusual story. It sets a pattern, gives us precepts and principles, not only for the remaining part of the book of Genesis but also for the entire inspired record that we call the Bible.

It talks about a **family**. The basic unit of our society is not the government, not society, not the church, but the family and the home. Since the family was here first, it has prior rights, prior obligations and prior responsibilities. The family is God's **first** love. Without the **family** there would be no church, no government and no society.

> **The family is God's first love.**

God is the God of the family, and the Bible is a family Book. Family relationships are important to God, to us, the church, the community, the nation and to the world.

This passage portrays the innermost feelings and interactions of one of the most famous families in all the Bible. Immediately, it is the family of Jacob. Historically, it is the family of Abraham. Ultimately, it becomes the family of Joseph.

Joseph was a patriarch. There are many things in this text and through these next few chapters that show how Joseph was a type of our Lord Jesus, but that is not the purpose of this study. Joseph was a patriarch, a type of Christ, one of the twelve sons of Jacob, a grandson of Isaac, and a great-grandson of Abraham.

What a rich heritage he had! What a marvelous background! What a wonderful family he came from! It was not a perfect family by any means.

The principal characters in this dramatic story are in basically three groups: (1) a gifted young man; (2) an aging father; and (3) eleven jealous brothers.

The gifted young man was Joseph. His brothers nick-named him "the dreamer." *Joseph* means "revealer of secrets." This says volumes about Joseph and his life, not only while he was at home, but after he was in Egypt, first as a prisoner and then as prime minister.

Doesn't God do some wonderful things? He can take a man out of prison and make him a prime minister. Isn't that something? When we see a man come out of prison, we are suspicious of him, and maybe rightly so; but every man deserves a second chance.

This combination—a gifted young son, an aging father and eleven jealous brothers—provides a perfect formula for a family squabble and a family fight. Sibling rivalry is not uncommon, nor is it new. It started a long time ago. It has been in the human race ever since Adam.

This family crisis centers around the gifted son. He is unusual, unique and misunderstood. Joseph is the son of his dad's old age. This makes him the fair-haired favorite boy. He gets anything he wants. This is where the trouble begins for Joseph and where it starts in any family.

Two things contribute to this dilemma: (1) the love of Jacob toward his son Joseph in giving him a coat of many colors, something he didn't give the other boys; (2) the jealousy of Joseph's brothers. This jealousy led to bitterness, hatred and foul play.

Let me issue a stern warning. An unkind act or attitude by any family member or any number of members can rock the foundation of family harmony. A family can be torn apart by the attitude or action of just one, to say nothing of eleven against one. The odds were totally stacked against Joseph.

In "A Family Shakeup," there are two major areas of thinking.

THE DREAMS OF JOSEPH

Before the written Word, God used dreams to get across a message. He does not speak in visions and dreams in this age. God has already spoken. He has given us the Bible. It has 66 separate volumes, 1,189 chapters. God has already said all He is going to say. He is never going to say anything beyond His revealed Word. He is never going to do anything contrary to His revealed Word. So don't look for any added revelation. Don't ask God to send you a dream from Heaven or a vision from above. He has quit speaking through dreams. In Joseph's day God did speak through dreams. So Joseph's dreams enter into this picture very prominently.

Joseph's first dream. Genesis 37:5–8 records the story of Joseph's first dream. When he told his brothers about it, it immediately incited hatred in their hearts. He actually relates it to them. I am paraphrasing a bit: 'I dreamed a dream. We were all out in a field binding sheaves. I had brought together a sheaf, and it stood straight up. You fellows brought your sheaves. They stood up, then bowed over to my sheaf.'

The interpretation is in verse 8: "And his brethren said to him, Shalt thou indeed reign over us?" They knew immediately what the dream meant—that Joseph would be elevated to a superior position over them, and they eventually would bow down in humble submission before him.

What were the consequences? We have seen the dream, we have seen the interpretation, now the consequences (vs. 5): ". . . and they hated him yet the more."

Notice the wording. They already hated him because he was the son of old age, the favorite son whom the father had given a coat of many colors. Now he comes up with this dream: 'Ultimately you will bow down before me and make obeisance to me.' " . . . And they hated him yet the more."

Joseph's second dream. Genesis 37:9–11 records Joseph's second dream. I am again going to paraphrase: 'Joseph dreamed yet another dream. Behold, the sun and the moon and eleven stars all made obeisance to me. My star shined above all the stars of heaven; and even the sun and the moon were in submission to my star, the light, the magnitude, the brightness of my light.'

What did that mean? That Joseph's family, including his mother and daddy and all eleven brothers, will one day be in submission to Joseph. This is all in God's plan and program.

Parents, something that is happening in your child's life while he or she is young could be a foretaste of what God has for that child ten, fifteen, twenty-five or forty years from now. So be careful how you stifle the development of your child when God is doing something in his or her life. Perhaps you don't understand it now, but when you can't understand, just learn to trust Him.

God has to have someone one day to be the pastor of this church. God has to have someone one day to be the president for this country. God has to have someone one day to be the mayor for this city. God has to have little children to grow up into men and women to give them places and positions of responsibility.

If your child acts a bit different from other children, be careful how you stifle him, how you criticize him, how you handle him. God may be working in that child's life in a way that will affect this whole nation.

The **consequences** of Joseph's second dream were inordinate jealousy and cruel envy. "And his brethren envied him." That word *"envy"* means they were ready, willing and desirous to hurt, harm, disturb and eventually to destroy.

Envy will destroy—not the one you are envious of, but **you**. It didn't destroy Joseph; it destroyed his brothers.

Acts 7:9 reads, "And the patriarchs [Joseph's brothers], moved with envy, sold Joseph into Egypt: but God was with him." His brothers thought this deed would prove to be Joseph's undoing. They had a design, a desire and a determination to destroy him, "but God was with him."

I say to you: Things may be happening in your life

which don't seem so profitable, so good, so wonderful. But if you are in God's will, obeying His Word, and following the Holy Spirit's leading, know that God is with you and is going to turn that which seems evil into good.

Before this story is finished, Joseph is going to say, 'You meant this for evil, but God meant it for good.' His brothers envied him and sold him into slavery, "but God was with him."

There can be family jealousy. Sadly enough, when a family member begins to prosper, or is promoted, or becomes prominent in the community, it sometimes causes a rift between him and the family. You have seen it. Everything goes along fine as long as we are all on the same level; but let one rise up a bit, get a good position, or head up a business or corporation, or get promoted, and the other members will say, "Who does he think he is?" They look on him with envy, jealousy and bitterness. The root of that rift is the green-eyed monster called jealousy.

We have a commentary on jealousy in Song of Solomon 8:6: "Set me as a seal upon thine heart, as a seal upon thine arm: for love is strong as death; jealousy is cruel as the grave: the coals thereof are coals of fire, which hath a most vehement flame."

Nothing is more destructive than jealousy. The wise Solomon said that jealousy is as cruel as the grave. It burns with a vehement heat. It is hot, it is destructive; it is damnable. It will destroy your home. Get that green-eyed monster under control.

There are reasons why you are jealous. I quote Dr. J. Frank Norris: "If you are jealous of somebody, that person has more than you have, knows more than you know, and can do more than you can do." Aren't you ashamed of yourself for admitting that anybody knows more than you know, has more than you have, and can do more than you can do?

There was jealousy in the first family, and the commentary is in Genesis 4:1–5:

"And Adam knew Eve his wife; and she conceived, and bare Cain, and said, I have gotten a man from the LORD.

"And she again bare his brother Abel. And Abel was a keeper of sheep, but Cain was a tiller of the ground.

"And in process of time it came to pass, that Cain brought of the fruit of the ground an offering unto the LORD.

"And Abel, he also brought of the firstlings of his flock and of the fat thereof.

"And the LORD had respect unto Abel and to his offering: But unto Cain and to his offering he had not respect. And Cain was very wroth, and his countenance fell."

Cain made up his mind that he was going to kill his brother. Cain's offering was rejected because it was of his own hands. Abel's offering was accepted because it was of the flock, a blood sacrifice.

The result was a family squabble, a family fight that ended in the first murder on record.

We have church jealousy. The same thing happens in a church family. When one member gains prominence over another, or gets more attention from the pulpit, believe it or not, even Christians, godly people who occupy a pew, give money, sing, teach and will preach, get jealous.

First Corinthians 3 is a biblical example of a church racked with and divided by jealousy. It is the most carnal church in the New Testament, and the major cause was jealousy.

"And I, brethren, could not speak unto you as unto spiritual, but as unto carnal, even as unto babes in Christ.

"I have fed you with milk, and not with meat: for hitherto ye were not able to bear it, neither yet now are ye able.

"For ye are yet carnal: for whereas there is among you envying, and strife, and divisions, are ye not carnal, and walk as men?

"For while one saith, I am of Paul; and another, I am of Apollos; are ye not carnal?"—I Cor. 3:1–4.

Divided by jealousy! "I belong to Paul's group. I belong to Apollos' group. This is my pew." Isn't it sad that there is jealousy and envy even in a church?

THE DEDICATION OF JOSEPH

In Genesis 37, verses 12 through 17, two things reveal the character and the dedication of Joseph. There are no more outstanding traits that a man could have than the two Joseph had.

Joseph complied with his father's instructions. Look at verse 13. Joseph, when his father said to him, 'I want to send you out to the field,' said, "Here am I." He was ready to go. What lesson are we to learn? Obedience to parents. Children, this message is for you as well as for Mother and Daddy. I am not talking about a husband and wife breakup; I am talking about children, talking about siblings, about what happens in a family with children. Children, obey your parents.

Ephesians 6:1–3:

"Children, obey your parents in the Lord: for this is right.

"Honour thy father and mother; which is the first commandment with promise;

"That it may be well with thee, and thou mayest live long on the earth."

Children, obey. You say, "I am eighteen, I don't have to obey." Who said so? Joseph was seventeen. Some of you, by the time you reach ten, eleven or twelve, think, *Hey, I am on my own. I can do what I want.* You cannot do what you want and get by with it. Young people, children, youth—seventeen, eighteen, nineteen, twenty, twenty-one—if you are still under your parents' roof, still under their care, don't you disobey them or talk back to them. Don't you refer to them as "the old man" and "the old woman." Don't you stand up and spit out something to either parent in a sassy and disrespectful manner. You do, and your kids will throw it back at YOU.

Be obedient to parents. Obey those in authority over you.

Joseph had concern for his brothers. Verses 15 through 17 contain a lesson to learn: he went looking for his brothers. He searched for them to find out how they were doing. The lesson here is **compassion** for our family, even if any one of them has used us or abused us.

Boys, girls, young people, don't ever say, "I hate you!" to your sister or your brother. If you do, those words will come back to haunt you someday. That word will never die; no word you verbalize will ever die. Sound is energy, and energy cannot be destroyed.

Boys flying kites can haul back their white-winged birds,
But you can't do that when you are flying words.
Thoughts unexpressed may fall back dead,
But not even God can change them, once they're said.

Be careful. Walls have ears. You and I may live long enough to see some kind of technology that will produce some kind of instrument that will pick up the Gettysburg Address or the Sermon on the Mount. Twenty years ago we didn't believe what they could do with computers. What will another twenty years bring forth? It blows my mind. I don't understand how we can put something in a machine and it gets to New York in three seconds. A few years ago we wouldn't have believed it. We believe it now because we see it every day.

I am saying, be careful. Compassion for your family is very important. Read Ephesians 4:30–32:

"And grieve not the holy Spirit of God, whereby ye are sealed unto the day of redemption.

"Let all bitterness, and wrath, and anger, and clamour, and evil speaking, be put away from you, with all malice:

"And be ye kind one to another, tenderhearted, forgiving one another, even as God for Christ's sake hath forgiven you."

"Pastor, does that mean my own fleshly brother?" Sure. It means your Christian brother and your own brother as well. We are warned, "Let all bitterness, and wrath, and anger, and clamour, and evil speaking, be put away from you, with all malice."

SOLUTIONS FOR A FAMILY SHAKEUP

When your family begins to show signs of a **shakeup**, don't wait until they **break up,** but incorporate the following five things:

You should diversify family devotions. What do I mean by that? Daddy, you say to little Johnny, "Tomorrow, Johnny, you are to read Psalm 1 in family devotions." You say to Susie, "Susie, you are to quote your favorite Bible story." You say to Jim, "Jim, you are to pray tomorrow in the family devotions."

That will bring about a spiritual bond in the family

that nothing else can. Daddy is in charge. Daddy is the head of the home. Daddy, diversify your family devotions. If you are not now having family devotions, start having them. Oh, I hear it all the time, "But pastor, I don't have time." Make time. Turn off the television earlier than you usually do so you can have family devotions—**diversify.**

You should intensify family togetherness. You can do this by planning more family activities. The family that plays together stays together. Take the family on a picnic. Go on a vacation together.

Probably you ought not go to New Orleans! My soul! Many years ago, my wife and I decided to see New Orleans. Guess where our hotel was located. On Bourbon Street, right in the heart of the most ungodly, depraved section. About 2:00 a.m. I said, "I hope Jesus doesn't come tonight. My soul! I don't want God to catch us in this place. This is like Sodom and Gomorrah. Honey, let's slip out of here. Let's not wait until day-break." So we got up and stole away.

You don't have to go to Hawaii or California. Pack a picnic lunch, go down the street to a park, and have a family outing—**intensify.**

You should amplify family favors. You can do this by performing a random act of kindness. Don't wait until a birthday, an anniversary or Christmas. Do a random act of kindness today. You might start by telling your wife how much you love her. (Give her a little warning; she might faint!) Or tell your children you love them.

When I was just a little lad, I would climb up on Daddy's lap. I used to love to feel Daddy's neck. Son, climb up on your daddy's lap, feel his neck and say, "Daddy, I love you." You say, "I'm sixteen and too big." You are never too big to do that. Daughter, climb up on your mother's lap and tell her you love her.

Random acts of kindness won't cost a thing—**amplify.**

You should rectify family differences. Family differences can be corrected in a family powwow. Just sit down and talk things out. Don't get in the bedroom and scream back to the kitchen or upstairs to the kids. Get them all together, sit down and then talk it out—**rectify.**

You should simplify family chores. This is easily done by working together to accomplish the chores of everyday life. Make work **fun** time. "Here, let me help you take out the trash. Let me help with the dishes. Let's work together. You wash and I'll dry." (Or do you dry dishes anymore?) Get the family together and make work a fun time, not a horrible time—**simplify.**

You can prevent a family **breakup** by properly handling a family **shakeup.** Don't wait until it becomes a point of no return.

There are three things that are absolutely necessary, and these govern the five solutions to a family shakeup that I have just given you:

- compassion;
- communication;
- commitment.

I call you to a rededication of your family before the **shakeup** comes; if the **shakeup** has already begun, then before the **breakup** comes.

A FAMILY BREAKUP

—JOSEPH—
Genesis 37:18–36

"And when they saw him afar off, even before he came near unto them, they conspired against him to slay him.

"And they said one to another, Behold, this dreamer cometh.

"Come now therefore, and let us slay him, and cast him into some pit, and we will say, Some evil beast hath devoured him: and we shall see what will become of his dreams.

"And Reuben heard it, and he delivered him out of their hands; and said, Let us not kill him.

"And Reuben said unto them, Shed no blood, but cast him into this pit that is in the wilderness, and lay no hand upon him; that he might rid him out of their hands, to deliver him to his father again.

"And it came to pass, when Joseph was come unto his brethren, that they stript Joseph out of his coat, his coat of many colours that was on him;

"And they took him, and cast him into a pit: and the pit was empty, there was no water in it.

"And they sat down to eat bread: and they lifted up their eyes and looked, and, behold, a company of Ishmeelites came from Gilead with their camels bearing spicery and balm and myrrh, going to carry it down to Egypt.

"And Judah said unto his brethren, What profit is it if we slay our brother, and conceal his blood?

"Come, and let us sell him to the Ishmeelites, and let not our hand be upon him; for he is our brother and our flesh. And his brethren were content.

"Then there passed by Midianites merchantmen; and they drew and lifted up Joseph out of the pit, and sold Joseph to the Ishmeelites for twenty pieces of silver: and they brought Joseph into Egypt.

"And Reuben returned unto the pit; and, behold, Joseph was not in the pit; and he rent his clothes.

"And he returned unto his brethren, and said, The child is not; and I, whither shall I go?

"And they took Joseph's coat, and killed a kid of the goats, and dipped the coat in the blood;

"And they sent the coat of many colours, and they brought it to their father; and said, This have we found: know now whether it be thy son's coat or no.

"And he knew it, and said, It is my son's coat; an evil beast hath devoured him; Joseph is without doubt rent in pieces.

"And Jacob rent his clothes, and put sackcloth upon his loins, and mourned for his son many days.

"And all his sons and all his daughters rose up to comfort him; but he refused to be comforted; and he said, For I will go down into the grave unto my son mourning. Thus his father wept for him.

"And the Midianites sold him into Egypt unto Potiphar, an officer of Pharaoh's, and captain of the guard."

The family of Jacob has come to a point in their history and in their relationships one with another that they have been shaken up. The shakeup came because of the love that Jacob had for his son Joseph, the son of the old age; the gift that he gave him; the coat of many colors, and the dreams Joseph dreamed.

This text reveals just how deep and destructive a family disagreement can be. The consequences are staggering. This family is literally torn apart, and the root cause is **jealousy**. Here is a dysfunctional family.

History is replete with examples of dysfunctional families. In fact, every family in Adam's race has dysfunctional characteristics as a result of the sin nature that we received when man disobeyed God.

There is no family that is not dysfunctional in some

way. The root of sin causes it. From time to time, it would be profitable for each family to take inventory of their relationships. Sometimes we tend to take for granted those nearest and dearest to us, those who have done the most for us. We tend to, even if not intentionally, carelessly and thoughtlessly mistreat them. So take inventory of your relationships and make any adjustments necessary to avert a catastrophe. Nothing is sadder than a family's being broken apart.

Let me suggest four questions to ask yourself in this inventory:

1. Am I the dedicated husband or wife that I should be to my spouse?

2. Am I a considerate, loving, thoughtful, caring parent?

3. Am I fair, equitable and honest in my dealings with my family members?

4. Do I take my family members for granted?

Young people, here are two questions to ask yourself:

1. Am I an obedient son or daughter?

2. In keeping with the instructions of God's Word, do I obey, honor and respect my parents?

There is not a soul who doesn't need to evaluate himself. If you are alone and have nobody in your immediate family, here are three questions to ask yourself:

1. Am I the person I ought to be?

2. What do my distant relatives think of me?

3. Have I treated them fairly? Have I been honest?

All of us should ask ourselves these questions as we consider averting or avoiding a family **shakeup** or ultimately a family **breakup**.

There are two major areas to consider in "A Family Breakup": the **conspiracy** (vss. 18–28) and the **cover-up** (vss. 31–36).

THE CONSPIRACY THAT CAUSED THE BREAKUP

There are six things about the conspiracy that I will name:

(1) The conspiracy was the result of family **jealousy**. Remember Joseph's dream, remember the coat of many colors, remember the reason they were jealous of Joseph. Jacob had a special love for Joseph that motivated him to make him a coat of many colors, causing the brothers to become jealous.

(2) The conspiracy was against an **innocent person**. What one thing did Joseph do that would cause his brothers to hate him so intensely? I know you are going to say, "He was the favorite son." That wasn't his fault. Joseph couldn't help being born. He couldn't help how his daddy felt toward him.

We have no record of Joseph's begging his father to do him any special favors. He certainly had nothing to do with being born the son of old age. He had nothing to do, humanly speaking, with the message that he gave his brothers which caused them to hate him intensely and become jealous of him. Joseph's earthly father loved him and showed him special favor.

The Father in Heaven gave him two dreams that not only affected an immediate family but the whole human race at that time in history. That was God's dealings. Joseph was innocent, so the conspiracy was against an innocent person.

114

(3) The conspiracy was an **act of cowardice**. The odds were ten to one. Those were difficult odds to be up against.

(4) The conspiracy included a **plot to murder** an innocent man. In verse 20 his brothers said, "Let us slay him." They conspired against him; now it has reached the point where they are ready to kill him.

(5) The conspiracy was changed from a plot to murder Joseph to a **plan to abandon** him to die of starvation. Reuben, the oldest, said, 'Let us not kill our brother. He is our flesh and blood. Let us just cast him into this pit.' Reuben was scheming to deliver Joseph from this awful fate. All agreed to follow Reuben's plan.

(6) The conspiracy ended in a **money-making scheme**. There was in Judah's heart the idea, 'What does it profit us if we kill him? Let us sell him and make a little extra money.'

Isn't it amazing what people will do for money! We occasionally read where a mother sells her baby for money, where men sell their wives for money, where women sell their bodies for money.

The **love** of money, not money itself, is the root of all evil. Money has no power within itself. Let me illustrate. A five-dollar bill has absolutely no evil or good power within itself. It just depends on how you use it. If you take a five-dollar bill and give it to a hungry person to buy food, the money has been used for something good. If you buy a case of beer, then the money becomes something evil. Money is neutral. Money has no good or bad quality. It depends on how you use it. The **love** of money is the root of all evil.

So we have seen the conspiracy of the brothers of Joseph against him.

THE COVER-UP OF THE CRIME

Now we come to the second major part, the cover-up of a crime, a crime against an innocent man. Two things about the cover-up:

(1) It was a **deliberate and dastardly deed** designed to deceive their daddy. They decided to kill an innocent animal, dip the coat in blood, take it back to Daddy and say, "This we found. Lo, is this thy son's coat?" The relationship has cooled off a bit more.

(2) The cover-up **broke the heart of an aging father**. Many a man has gone down to his grave mourning the loss of a son! God intervened, and it didn't happen in this case; Jacob thought he was going to his grave still mourning his son's fate.

How many times has that actually happened! A daddy has gone to a grave, sometimes an early grave, feeling remorse, sorrow, grief and pain because of a tragedy that happened, a tragedy that might have been averted.

Here they are in this cover-up, breaking their father's heart. Verse 34 says, "Jacob rent [or tore] his clothes." He "put sackcloth upon his loins, and mourned for his son many days." Even when the sons tried to comfort him, he said, "For I will go down into the grave unto my son mourning."

Now I share some thoughts with you about breakups and their price.

TOO BIG A PRICE TO PAY

The price is far too high to pay, and life is too short for you to cause a rift in your family. Breakups result in **hurtful scars** that are difficult to heal; some of them never

116

heal. Family breakups result in **broken hearts** that are a long time mending, and some never mend. Breakups result in **estranged feelings** that make reconciliation a slow process.

Some of you are going to say, "Dr. Barber, there is a rift in my family. I have a sister (brother, uncle, aunt, mother or daddy) to whom I do not speak."

Regardless of whose fault it is, have you sincerely done everything possible to mend that rift, to prevent that breakup, that division, in your family? If not, do it. Wouldn't it be nice to lie down at night with a clear conscience, knowing you have done everything that you can do to patch up a bad situation? When you stand before the God of the universe, you will be able to tell Him, "I did my best to make it right."

God is deeply concerned about families. Any division, any disruption, any rift, any problem, any shaking up or breaking up of your family grieves the heart of God because He is the **originator** and **designer** of the family.

It didn't just happen that way. God made man in His own image, then He caused a deep sleep to come upon man; and out of his body He took the rib from which He made the woman, and He put them together. He didn't take a part of the man's **head** so he could lord it over the woman: "I am the king of this castle." If you have to keep reminding your wife and your kids, "I am the head of this house," then you are not; you just think you are. He didn't take it out of Adam's **foot** so he could step on Eve. He took it from near his **heart** so they could be joined in a very special relationship.

This portrays the relationship between Christ and the church. (Look at Paul's writing in Ephesians 5.) God placed each of us in a family. He loves your family and doesn't want it to break up.

STEPS TO PREVENT A FAMILY BREAKUP

Some are going to say, "Pastor, we never have an argument"; or, "Pastor, we are so solid that we could never be pulled apart."

Wait just a minute! The Devil is out to do everything he can to turn children against parents, parents against children, husbands against wives, wives against husbands, because he knows that the strength of the family is the strength of the church and the nation. God's plan is to keep the family together. So don't think you are immune to temptations. Don't involve yourself in something that will end in disaster in your life, in your family, and in your home. If it has never happened, get down on your knees and thank God and pray that He will keep it from happening.

> **Family togetherness prevents family separateness.**

Family **togetherness** prevents family **separateness**.

Each of the following five things is very important to prevent a family breakup:

Cultivate dialogue among family members. Nothing is more important than communication. It is the one thing that will hold a family together.

The whole creation as we know it was brought into existence by a word. Ten times in Genesis 1 the Bible says, "And God said." It was the voice of God that brought into existence the material universe. Ultimately God said, "Let us make man in our image."

It was the voice of God that said, "Let there be light: and there was light."

It was the voice of God that said, "Let there be a firmament in the midst of the waters, and let it divide the waters from the waters. And God made the firmament, and divided the waters which were under the firmament from the waters which were above the firmament: and it was so."

It was God who said, "Let the waters bring forth abundantly the moving creature that hath life . . . . And God created great whales, and every living creature that moveth, which the waters brought forth abundantly . . . and God saw that it was good."

I am saying, you must communicate. Even your existence and everything in your material universe were brought about by the word of God. It was Jesus who said, "Man shall not live by bread alone, but by every word that proceedeth out of the mouth of God" (Matt. 4:4).

Paul says, "So then faith cometh by hearing, and hearing by the word of God" (Rom. 10:17). Even your salvation comes from the spoken Word. So cultivate dialogue among family members.

Proverbs 12:15 says, "But he that hearkeneth unto counsel is wise." I say that it is necessary for families to engage in communication. It should not be a monologue but a dialogue—an exchange of ideas and thoughts.

Proverbs 15:1 says, "A soft answer turneth away wrath: but grievous words stir up anger." I recommend that you season your words with love and compassion. Many times it is not **what** we say that hurts, but **how** we say it.

> There is power in the spoken word.

Proverbs 15:23 says, "A man hath joy by the answer of

his mouth: and a word spoken in due season, how good is it!" The right word spoken at the right time, in the right spirit, will likely prevent a family breakup. Communication is important.

Proverbs 25:15 says, "A soft tongue breaketh the bone." There is power in the spoken word. That old saying, "Sticks and stones may break my bones, but words can never hurt me," is not true. Words can hurt. Even a soft word can break a bone.

I repeat: there is **power** in the spoken word!

Conquer envy before it influences your behavior. Jealous thoughts lead to wicked conduct. What you **think,** you **do.** Your thoughts are translated into deeds. James gives us a commentary in his third chapter, verse 16: "For where envying and strife is, there is confusion and every evil work."

Control anger before it manifests itself in foul play. Unbridled, uncontrolled anger results in vicious actions. People do things when they are angry that they would never do if they were not angry. We do not know how many cars are wrecked and how many people are killed in automobiles because the driver got mad at someone in the car, turned his head to tell him off, and ran into a bridge abutment, another car or a telephone pole.

Anger expressed **verbally** sometimes hurts as much as anger expressed **physically.** Control your anger before it demonstrates your feelings in foul play. Proverbs 27:4 is the commentary: "Wrath is cruel, and anger is outrageous; but who is able to stand before envy?"

Consider the feelings of others before expressing your own. Before you bring a railing accusation against a member of your family, or speak an unkind, thoughtless word, ask yourself, *How will this affect him or her? What will be the consequences? How will it register in his or her heart? How will it affect the rest of my family?* Consider your **family's** feelings before you express your **own**. Romans 12:10 commands, "Be kindly affectioned one to another with brotherly love; in honour preferring one another."

Concentrate on the good and cancel out the bad. Before you say, "This is the worst thing I ever heard," or, "I hate you for this," before you pass judgment on the behavior of a family member, reflect on one good thing that family member has done for you, and it will change your attitude. After all, **your attitude** is the problem. A stinking attitude, wrong feelings, wrong thoughts ultimately become vicious deeds.

Here is a commentary in Philippians 4:8: "Finally, brethren, whatsoever things are true, whatsoever things are honest, whatsoever things are just, whatsoever things are pure, whatsoever things are lovely, whatsoever things are of good report; if there be any virtue, and if there be any praise, think on these things."

An added thought: Major on things that **unite** rather than on things that **divide** your family. "A stitch in time saves nine."

Do something about it **now**. **Wake up** before there is a **breakup**. Wake up and see what is happening in your family before it is too late.

In thirty-five years in the pastorate I have observed family members gather around a casket. One stands over here, one stands over there, one is in the back. They won't even gather together at the casket because of hard feelings. I have seen family members weep, some because they have done something wrong to the one in the casket. I have witnessed it. I have heard people beg their deceased loved one to forgive them. Now it is too late.

Do what is necessary to prevent a breakup in your family. If you see the least inkling of it, get your family at an altar, and ask God to help you prevent this from happening. It will take grace.

Someone somewhere needs you to call him or her and say, "I'm sorry. Please forgive me"; or there may be a family member that you need to put your arm around and say, "Let's pray about it."

Wake up before the **breakup**!

A FAMILY MAKEUP

—JOSEPH—
Genesis 45:1–15

"Then Joseph could not refrain himself before all them that stood by him; and he cried, Cause every man to go out from me. And there stood no man with him, while Joseph made himself known unto his brethren.

"And he wept aloud: and the Egyptians and the house of Pharaoh heard.

"And Joseph said unto his brethren, I am Joseph; doth my father yet live? And his brethren could not answer him; for they were troubled at his presence.

"And Joseph said unto his brethren, Come near to me, I pray you. And they came near. And he said, I am Joseph your brother, whom ye sold into Egypt.

"Now therefore be not grieved, nor angry with yourselves, that ye sold me hither: for God did send me before you to preserve life.

"For these two years hath the famine been in the land: and yet there are five years, in the which there shall neither be earing nor harvest.

"And God sent me before you to preserve you a posterity in the earth, and to save your lives by a great deliverance.

"So now it was not you that sent me hither, but God: and he hath made me a father to Pharaoh, and lord of all his house, and a ruler throughout all the land of Egypt.

"Haste ye, and go up to my father, and say unto him, Thus saith thy son Joseph, God hath made me lord of all Egypt: come down unto me, tarry not:

"And thou shalt dwell in the land of Goshen, and thou shalt be near unto me, thou, and thy children, and thy children's children, and thy flocks, and thy herds, and all that thou hast:

"And there will I nourish thee; for yet there are five years of famine; lest thou, and thy household, and all that thou hast, come to poverty.

"And, behold, your eyes see, and the eyes of my brother Benjamin, that it is my mouth that speaketh unto you.

"And ye shall tell my father of all my glory in Egypt, and of all that ye have seen; and ye shall haste and bring down my father hither.

"And he fell upon his brother Benjamin's neck, and wept; and Benjamin wept upon his neck.

"Moreover he kissed all his brethren, and wept upon them: and after that his brethren talked with him."

What a marvelous story! The years have come and gone since Joseph was a lad in his father's household and since the time his father sent him out with a coat of many colors to discover the well-being of his brothers. The favorite son became the target of evil-minded, cruel brothers.

The tables have turned. Joseph has now become the prime minister of the greatest country in the world at that time, the most populated and the richest nation with the most bountiful crops.

You remember the program that Joseph recommended to Pharaoh. God gave Joseph wisdom to say, "This is the way we can prevent people from starving to death."

We need to get back to the Bible way of doing things. We need to get back to God's plan, God's pattern, God's program for our lives individually, for our churches and for our nation.

Joseph now has come through a **prison**, through a false **accusation**, through a terrifying pit **experience** by his own brothers, sold to strangers, into Egypt, into a prison; now he is the prime minister.

The time has come for a family reunion. There is no joy like the joy of coming together in a reunion and a reconciliation. The coming together of a family that has been torn apart by jealousy and strife, discord and envy is one of the sweetest experiences we can know. The story of Joseph and his brothers is a perfect example.

God ordained that there be harmony in the home. It is not the plan nor purpose of God that families be broken apart and torn asunder. They should be together with love, compassion and understanding one for another. My soul, how wonderful it is to have the love of your family! How marvelous for families to share together!

The consequences of this story did not end at the borders of Egypt or at the mainland of Israel. This story has nationwide and worldwide consequences. God was working out a plan for His people, Israel. He had in mind that He would bring a people into existence, the great nation of Israel, the seed of Abraham, Isaac and Jacob, that out of their loins and out of the loins of the great King David would come One who would rule all the world. They called Him Jesus, the Saviour of all mankind.

God always works according to a **plan** and **program**. God is using things we don't understand, things that are baffling, imponderable, indescribable, indefinable to us, to formulate a program.

> God always works according to a plan and program.

This family affected the whole nation of Israel, Egypt and, ultimately, every nation under the shining sun. As goes the nation Israel, so goes the world—the Arab-Israel conflict in the Middle East, the drawing of the lines, the peace parties, the peace gatherings, the peace talks, the war and strife and down to our day.

There is yet a future unfolding of God's plan of the ages. Once this great church age has come to a close and the last Gentile believer has been saved, the trumpet will sound, the dead in Christ will rise, Jesus will return, and the rapture will take place. That awesome period known as "the time of Jacob's trouble" will then follow.

This is the reason God is keeping this family intact. They have had their differences, but God is bringing them back together. The great period of Tribulation, "the time of Jacob's trouble," is the time during which God will refine that nation and get it ready for the greatest blessing they have ever had—the great kingdom.

So first comes Tribulation, then Armageddon. What is all of this about? It is about who Israel is and where Israel is. God fights for Israel. Zechariah 14:2 says, "For I will gather all nations against Jerusalem to battle." The Bible says that Jesus will intervene, the Lord will intervene, God will intervene. There will be a great battle, the battle of Armageddon, when all the forces of the earth are gathered in array against the Son of God. With the brightness of His coming and the sword that goes out of His mouth, even His word, He will destroy all nations of earth. Then comes the kingdom of peace, prosperity and productivity, all under the reign and the domain of Jesus Christ who comes out of the loins of Abraham, Isaac, Jacob and King David.

An ancient proverb says:

> If there is righteousness in the heart,
> There will be beauty in the character.
> If there is beauty in the character,
> There will be harmony in the home.
> If there is harmony in the home,

There will be order in the nation.
If there is order in the nation,
There will be peace in the world.

Your family relationships will not likely directly affect the policy of America nor affect the world at large. But the status, the condition, the spiritual temperature of your family will affect the people around you.

Other families are watching your family. Other families need your family. They need an example, a prototype, a pattern, a model. Other families are either directly or indirectly influenced by what your family does.

So it is important that you muster your strength, everything that it takes, whatever it takes, to keep your family in tune with God.

Many a marriage could be salvaged, many a home could be saved, if people would follow the divinely inspired example of Joseph and his brothers. No rift is too wide, no chasm is too deep, no mountain is too high, no valley is too expansive but what the grace of God is sufficient to meet the need.

My friend, God is far more concerned about your family and its relationships than you could possibly imagine. A family that had a **shakeup** goes on to have a **breakup**, but, thank God, there can be a **makeup**!

In our study on "A Family Makeup," there are three things we will look at: the **providence** of God, the **provision** of grace, and the **prominence** of glory.

THE PROVIDENCE OF GOD

I call three things to your attention in the providence of God:

The providence of God sent Joseph into Egypt to preserve the nation of Israel. I will paraphrase verse 5: 'Be not grieved, nor angry, nor upset with yourself; be not disturbed, distressed, nor bothered; for God did send me before you to preserve life.'

Now read verses 7 and 8:

"And God sent me before you to preserve you a posterity in the earth, and to save your lives by a great deliverance.

"So now it was not you that sent me hither, but God: and he hath made me a father to Pharaoh, and lord of all his house, and a ruler throughout all the land of Egypt."

God sent Joseph to preserve a nation, to preserve a people. Could we apply that to our Joseph, Jesus Christ? God sent our Joseph, Jesus Christ, into the world to save His people. John 3:16 clearly states: "For God so loved the world, that he gave his only begotten Son, that whosoever believeth in him should not perish, but have everlasting life."

The providence of God placed Joseph in a prominent position in the land of Egypt. Verse 8 states, "So now it was not you that sent me hither, but God: and he hath made me a father to Pharaoh, and lord of all his house, and a ruler throughout all the land of Egypt." Could we apply that to Jesus, our Joseph? One day God will send Jesus Christ again to this world as King and Lord. John writes in Revelation 19:11–16:

"And I saw heaven opened, and behold a white horse; and he that

sat upon him was called Faithful and True, and in righteousness he doth judge and make war.

"His eyes were as a flame of fire, and on his head were many crowns; and he had a name written, that no man knew, but he himself.

"And he was clothed with a vesture dipped in blood: and his name is called The Word of God.

"And the armies which were in heaven followed him upon white horses, clothed in fine linen, white and clean.

"And out of his mouth goeth a sharp sword, that with it he should smite the nations: and he shall rule them with a rod of iron: and he treadeth the winepress of the fierceness and wrath of Almighty God.

"And he hath on his vesture and on his thigh a name written, KING OF KINGS, AND LORD OF LORDS."

That is my Lord and Saviour! He is not just an ordinary fellow: He is the King of kings, He is the Lord of lords, He is the Commandant of commandants, He is the Major of all majors, He is the Captain of our salvation, He is prominent, He has preeminence. He is the Lord of Glory, of Heaven and earth. What a wonderful Messianic type is Joseph!

The providence of God brought Joseph's family to the place where Joseph was. Look at verse 9: "Haste ye, and go up to my father, and say unto him, Thus saith thy son Joseph, God hath made me lord of all Egypt: come down unto me, tarry not."

One day Jesus will come, and He will sound His voice. When the trumpet sounds, the voice of God and the voice of the archangel will be heard; the trumpet of God shall sound, and the dead shall rise.

In John 14:1–3 Jesus made us this promise before He went away:

"Let not your heart be troubled: ye believe in God, believe also in me.

"In my Father's house are many mansions: if it were not so, I would have told you. I go to prepare a place for you.

"And if I go and prepare a place for you, I will come again, and receive you unto myself; that where I am, there ye may be also."

Joseph wanted all his family gathered around him. Our Joseph wants all His family gathered around Him in Heaven. We will have mansions, and there will be a street of gold, gates of pearl, walls of jasper—all prepared by God's Son, for God's family.

Oh, when God's family gets together in our Home above, there will be no dysfunctional members. All family members will be perfect: no family squabbles, no feuding, no fussing, no fighting, no difference, no discord, no distractions, all because of the providence of God to send our Joseph to preserve us, to be the King of kings. Our Joseph will bring us nearer to Him.

THE PROVISION OF GRACE

Look at verse 6: "For these two years hath the famine been in the land: and yet there are five years, in the which there shall neither be earing nor harvest." Five more years of famine, while the grace of God through Joseph would insure provision.

> God works through individuals.

Watch this: God works through individuals. He doesn't bless machines, denominations, fellowships or conferences. He blesses men. The grace of God through Joseph supplied the needs of the people for the duration of the famine.

Oh, the wonders, the marvelous wonders of God's grace!

His grace **sweetens** the bitter waters of adversity.

His grace **heals** the breach between Himself and a sinful man.

His grace **lightens** the load of life's heavy burdens.

His grace **narrows** the gap between friend and foe.

His grace **calms** the storms that threaten our lives.

His grace **salves** the sores caused by sin's corruption.

His grace **fathoms** the depths of man's depression and degradation.

His grace **solves** the problems that separate families.

His grace **brings** together those who have been torn apart.

We will understand better by and by that the grace of God has supplied every need that we ever had. "But my God shall supply all your need according to his riches in glory by Christ Jesus"—not according to our riches, but according to His. He has it all. He owns it all— "according to his riches in glory."

If you miss everything else, don't miss this important thought: God works through **adversity** to bring us from where we are to where He wants us to be in His divinely planned program.

God works through troublous times, through difficulties, through heartaches and through trials. This was a tremendous trial for Joseph. Think about this young boy in a pit where he easily could have starved to death. Think about him in a strange land, sold to the Midianites who carried him to Egypt and made more money off of him. As a young lad, he is working as a slave in the household of Potiphar, an officer of Pharaoh.

Potiphar's wife tries to trap him. He escapes. She

falsely accuses him. He spends a couple of years in prison. Think about his adversity, his hardship, his trial.

All the while, God is working out a plan, a program that is not only affecting Joseph's family, the nation of Israel and the nation of Egypt, but is affecting you. You are in this, I am in this, we are all in this because God is preserving the nation of Israel to bless all of the nations of earth through Jesus Christ.

So when you are going through that difficulty, when it looks as if you are going all downhill and there seems to be no end to your adversities, remember that the great Weaver is weaving a pattern for your life. The great Architect is designing a building for your life. He who is in control of everything holds you in His unchanging hand.

Though you may not see God's plan today, tomorrow, the next day, or next week, you **will** see it, for God will show you. He will one day make all things plain.

> My Father's way may twist and turn,
> My heart may throb and ache,
> But in my soul I'm glad I know
> He maketh no mistake.
>
> My cherished plans may go astray,
> My hopes may fade away,
> But still I'll trust my Lord to lead,
> For He doth know the way.
>
> Tho' night be dark and it may seem
> That day will never break,
> I'll pin my faith, my all in Him;
> He maketh no mistake.
>
> There's so much now I cannot see,
> My eyesight's far too dim;

But come what may, I'll simply trust
And leave it all to Him.

For by and by the mist will lift,
And plain it all He'll make.
Through all the way, tho' dark to me,
He made not one mistake.

—A. M. Overton

We are not always on a level plane or on a straight shot. Sometimes we have to make a detour down a valley or up a hill. One day He will make it plain. When all the mist has rolled away and tears no longer flow, He will make it plain. God works through adversity to bring us from where we are to where we ought to be and where He wants us to be in His program. Get comfort from Psalm 119:71: 'It is good for me that I have been afflicted; that I might learn thy statutes."

Sometimes we are so busy, so rushed, so bothered, so bogged down, have so many things to do that the Bible is about the last thing we handle at night.

What am I saying? The psalmist said, 'It was a good thing that I had some problems in my life, that I suffered adversity.' What problems? We don't know. Maybe he was flat on his back and couldn't get up, or maybe he was sick or a shut-in. Maybe he had a serious family problem. Whatever it was, it drove him to the Word of God. He said, 'It was good to suffer affliction so I might learn the Scripture.'

THE PROMINENCE OF GLORY

We have seen the **providence of God**, the **provision of grace**; now let's look at the **prominence of glory**. Look at verse 13: "And ye shall tell my father of all my glory in Egypt." That little boy for whom he made a coat of many colors is now wearing the robe of royalty in Egypt. He is the prime minister. He has charge of all the food. Nobody could get anything to eat but those who came to Joseph.

I know a story so much better than that. My Joseph is in charge of the bread of life, and nobody gets a bite until he comes to Jesus who said, "I am the bread of life."

What a beautiful typology! "Tell my father of all my glory."

One of these days the glory of Jesus will be seen not only by the Father (as it was in the world before He ever came to humble Himself as a man and die on a cross), but by the whole human race. Habakkuk 2:14 reads, 'For the earth shall be filled with the knowledge of the glory of the LORD, as the waters cover the sea."

Everything I have talked about comes right back to one thing and one theme—a family makeup. Wonderful things will happen when your family makes up. Let me give you now a **formula**. Everything I am going to say is backed up by a verse of Scripture right out of this chapter.

THINGS THAT WILL BRING ABOUT A FAMILY MAKEUP

Arrange a suitable environment for a family get-together. Not just any place or any circumstance or any environment will do. Look again at Genesis 45:1–3. What did Joseph do? He ordered everybody out—'Get all the strangers, all the Egyptians, all the worldlings out of here.' Nobody stood before him but his brothers.

A family cannot **get** together until they first **come**

together. Get the family together in the right environment, not with the television blaring nor with a thousand things going on but in a quiet place of solitude. No neighbors, no friends are there—just you, the family and God.

Acknowledge the plan and purpose of God in the operation of your family affairs. If you leave God out, then it is all over. You and I ought not make one purchase, one plan, go one place, do one thing, have one family activity, buy anything, sell anything, rent anything, do anything unless we bring God into it. He is interested in the family. Our families cannot survive, prosper or be happy apart from God.

Look again at verse 5, then verse 8.

In verse 5, Joseph says to his brothers, "Now therefore be not grieved, nor angry with yourselves [he detected their anger among themselves], that ye sold me hither: for God did send me before you to preserve life."

Verse 8 says, "So now it was not you that sent me hither, but God." Joseph's brothers sold him to Egypt, but God sent him to Egypt.

God has a plan for those circumstances now transpiring in your life. God has a purpose for those things that you don't quite understand. Romans 8:28 just jumps right off that page: "And we know that all things work together for good to them that love God, to them who are the called **according to his purpose.**"

Appeal to the best interests of the family by respecting the head of the family. God put the husband and father in the family unit as the head of the family. I know that many things have distorted, disturbed and destroyed that, but I am talking about the way it **ought** to be. God put the man, the father, at the head of the home. In verses 9, 10 and 11, Joseph said to his brothers, 'Make haste and go back. Say to my father that God has made me the lord of all Egypt. Hurry up and come down.' What did Joseph do?

He acknowledged, respected and honored his father.

Young people, no matter how old you are, if you live at home or don't live at home, honor and respect the authority of the head of that home. God will bless you for that.

> God honors children who honor their parents.

Appeal to the best interest of your family by respecting the head of the family. God honors children who honor their parents. "Honour thy father and thy mother: that thy days may be long upon the land which the LORD thy God giveth thee." Respect authority.

Allow a free and uninhibited expression of love and affection among family members. Look at verse 14 and through the first part of 15: "And he fell upon his brother Benjamin's neck, and wept; and Benjamin wept upon his neck. Moreover he kissed all his brethren, and wept upon them." These are the same brothers who put him in a pit, who sold him to the Midianites; the same brothers who hated him, who killed an animal, dipped his coat in the blood, sent the coat back to their daddy and asked, 'Is this your son's coat? Some wild animal must have devoured him.' Joseph fell on their necks and kissed them as he wept.

The prime minister weeping? Don't be ashamed of tears. In this day of macho-manhood, don't feel that only a baby cries. Crying is good for all. If you don't know how to cry, pinch yourself hard or do something else to yourself to make yourself cry. Look in the mirror, and then you will start crying! Learn how to cry if you don't know how to cry. The one person I know who could not cry died a bitter old man.

There is no shame in tears. The prime minister of Egypt wept. Jesus looked over the city of Jerusalem and wept. Allow an uninhibited, free and open expression of love and affection.

Accept the verbal input of the offenders in the case. Who were the offenders? The brothers had insulted Joseph; they had stolen his dignity. Anybody who is sold as a slave has his dignity taken away.

But look at the last part of verse 15, ". . . and after that his brethren talked with him."

Even the worst offender deserves his day in court. These men are in court; they are on trial. They deserve an opportunity to express themselves.

That brings me to a final scene. Look for two things in Genesis 50:15–21, the **confession** that Joseph's brothers made and the **concession** that Joseph made:

"And when Joseph's brethren saw that their father was dead, they said, Joseph will peradventure hate us, and will certainly requite us all the evil which we did unto him. [Are you beginning to see something?]

"And they sent a messenger unto Joseph, saying, Thy father did command before he died, saying,

"So shall ye say unto Joseph, Forgive, I pray thee now, the trespass of thy brethren, and their sin; for they did unto thee evil: and now, we pray thee, forgive the trespass of the servants of the God of thy father. And Joseph wept when they spake unto him.

"And his brethren also went and fell down before his face; and they said, Behold, we be thy servants.

"And Joseph said unto them, Fear not: for am I in the place of God? ['Is it up to me to forgive your sins? Am I God?']

"But as for you, ye thought evil against me; but God meant it unto good, to bring to pass, as it is this day, to save much people alive. Now therefore fear ye not: I will nourish you, and your little ones. And he comforted them, and spake kindly unto them."

First, the brothers had to **confess**. Before you and God, before you and the church, before you and your family can have a family makeup, you have to confess your sins.

Then Joseph conceded to do what was right: 'Fear not, fellows. I will nourish you, take care of you and your children.' He spake kindly to them and wept.

From then on, the family that had been **shaken up**, the family that had suffered a **breakup**, is now enjoying a **makeup**.

I appeal to your heart. If there is anything that drives a wedge between you and the Heavenly Father or anything that brings a division between you and a member of your family, go to an altar and settle it all. Have a family **makeup**. God wants that more than you can imagine!

For a complete list of books available from the Sword of the Lord, write to Sword of the Lord Publishers, P. O. Box 1099, Murfreesboro, Tennessee 37133.